THE STONES RIVER
AND
TULLAHOMA
CAMPAIGNS

CHRISTOPHER L. KOLAKOWSKI

Series Editor Douglas Bostick

THE
History
PRESS

Published by The History Press
Charleston, SC 29403
www.historypress.net

Copyright © 2011 by Christopher L. Kolakowski
All rights reserved

Cover image: Battle of Stone River Near Murfreesborough, Tenn., by Kurz and Allison. *Library of Congress.*

First published 2011

Manufactured in the United States

ISBN 978.1.59629.075.4

Library of Congress Cataloging-in-Publication Data

Kolakowski, Christopher L.
The Stones River and Tullahoma campaigns : this army does not retreat / Christopher L.
Kolakowski.
p. cm.
Includes bibliographical references.
ISBN 978-1-59629-075-4
1. Stones River, Battle of, Murfreesboro, Tenn., 1862-1863. 2. Tullahoma Region (Tenn.)-
-History, Military--19th century. 3. Tennessee--History--Civil War, 1861-1865--Campaigns.
4. United States--History--Civil War, 1861-1865--Campaigns. I. Title.
E474.77.K67 2011
973.7'33--dc23
2011036375

For
Corporal Oswald Babler, 46th Wisconsin Infantry
Private R. Bailey Schoonover, 21st Wisconsin Infantry
Army of the Cumberland

Who fought their war in Middle Tennessee
And their comrades who lie there still

Contents

Acknowledgements

G rowing up in Virginia, one quickly becomes aware of the Civil War and what it means to both the state and the entire country. The campaigns and battles of the Army of the Potomac and the Army of Northern Virginia permeate so much of northern and eastern Virginia that it is hard to escape. For some people, Virginia is the entire Civil War; but thanks to my Wisconsin relatives who fought in Middle Tennessee, I have always had an appreciation for the war in the West. Indeed, a study of the Western Theater often gives additional perspective and magnification to the war in the East. As a teenager, I latched on to the dramatic battles between the Army of the Cumberland and the Army of Tennessee, especially their colorful characters and portrayals of gallantry against high odds. Yet I also instinctively sensed their importance to the Civil War. I first visited the battlefields in 2000 and had my impressions confirmed. I have since returned many times. When The History Press gave me an opportunity to write the stories of Stones River and Tullahoma, I leaped at it.

Although my name appears on the cover of this book, this work would not have been possible without the help of others. First and foremost, recognition goes to Jim Lewis of Stones River National Battlefield, Greg Biggs and Mike Bradley. They contributed in ways large and small to my understanding of the war in Middle Tennessee and spent much time on visits and correspondence with me discussing these key operations. This book is far better for their input.

Others who contributed to this project include Kurt Holman of Perryville Battlefield State Historic Site, Matt Rector of U.S. Army Garrison at Fort Knox, Jim Ogden of Chickamauga and Chattanooga National Military

Park, Kevin Hymel, the staff at the Cowan Railroad Museum, Paul Harmon, J.D. Carruthers, Phil Seyfrit and Dave Powell. Great thanks is also due to Terry, Shirley and Elizabeth Woodson, who hosted me on several trips to Tennessee and took some great photos that appear in this book. I also would like to thank The History Press and my commissioning editor, Will McKay, who was a pleasure to work with on a second title in the publisher's Civil War Sesquicentennial Series. Any and all errors in this work are mine alone.

Active preservation movements are working to preserve and interpret the key sites associated with the Civil War in Tennessee. For more information and links, please visit www.tncivilwar.org.

Introduction

Nearly 40 percent of the Civil War's engagements occurred in Tennessee. The Volunteer State's strategic location between Kentucky and the Deep South ensured that it would be a major battleground. Two key rivers, the Cumberland and the Tennessee, provided good axes of advance for Union forces into the Confederacy. Deeply divided, men from Tennessee served on both sides during the war. Tennessee hosted many important battles, from Fort Donelson and Shiloh in 1862 to Franklin and Nashville in 1864. Nashville, the state capital, fell to the United States in February 1862 and thereafter became an important base for later operations against the Confederacy.

Both sides recognized Tennessee's importance and committed significant resources to this theater of operations. Each nation fielded its second-largest army in Middle Tennessee, the Union Army of the Cumberland and the Confederate Army of Tennessee. Dominating both sides' strategies was possession of the city of Chattanooga and its key rail junction, the vital link to Atlanta and the Deep South. The Federal forces sought to push down the strategic axis of the Nashville and Chattanooga Railroad through Chattanooga into Georgia, while the Confederates fought to halt and reverse the blue tide. Their failure to do so hastened the end of the war.

From November 1862 to July 1863, both sides engaged in intense operations in Middle Tennessee that exercised a profound impact on the Civil War. The opposing armies fought the war's bloodiest battle (by percentage of loss) at Stones River as 1862 turned to 1863. After a spring interlude, they clashed again during the Tullahoma Campaign in June and July 1863, which resulted in total Union control of Middle Tennessee. The Stones River and

Tullahoma operations were often overshadowed by more famous battles in the East or along the Mississippi River, but they played an equally important part in the war's course. Confederate seeds of mistrust and division planted in Middle Tennessee later bore fruit in the fall of 1863. After Tullahoma, the Federals controlled the gateway to Chattanooga, with all its possibilities. The decisive campaigns of Chickamauga, Chattanooga and Atlanta would have been impossible without Stones River and Tullahoma.

Chapter 1

War Comes to Tennessee

Decherd, Tennessee, shimmered in the summer heat of August 1862. A small way station along the Nashville and Chattanooga Railroad, its population swelled with an influx of Union soldiers. Although some of the locals welcomed these men in blue, the vast majority of Tennesseans in this area proved fervently pro-secessionist. The area buzzed with Federal infantry and wagons moving about. Significant activity centered on the headquarters of Major General Don Carlos Buell, the dour commander of the Army of the Ohio. Surrounded by staff and couriers, Buell headquartered in Decherd and prepared to strike at Chattanooga. If he could capture this key city before autumn, he would hold a dagger thrust against the vitals of the Confederacy.[1]

The Ohio-born Buell was a West Point graduate and a veteran of the Mexican-American War. After holding command in the Army of the Potomac for a short time, he had come west in the fall of 1861 and assumed command of the Army of the Ohio. Buell was a taciturn man who tried (not always successfully) to enforce tight Regular Army discipline on the volunteer regiments in his command. Like his patron George B. McClellan, Buell saw war in terms of armies moving in a vacuum, with little interference from politicians or effect on the civilians in their area of operations. This conservative view especially extended to the question of slavery and was enhanced by his family's ties to the South and slave-owning society. Because of this, General Buell also faced nagging and unfair doubts about his loyalty to the United States.[2]

As Buell and his staff examined the maps in front of them, their prospects seemed promising. For the past eight months, Federal armies had won an

Don Carlos Buell. *Perryville Battlefield State Historic Site.*

unbroken string of victories in the West. Now their forces were sprawled all over much of Tennessee, northern Mississippi and northern Alabama. Major General Ulysses S. Grant's Army of the Tennessee operated between Nashville and Memphis, while Buell's Army of the Ohio occupied most of Middle Tennessee between Nashville and the Cumberland Plateau outside Chattanooga. At that moment, Buell's Federals were slowly advancing toward Chattanooga, gateway to Atlanta and the Southern heartland. The war in the West appeared to be nearing a major turning point.[3]

The path of war in the Western Theater had been full of dramatic twists and turns up to this point. Tennessee and Kentucky proved to be the key pivot points. When North and South divided in the winter of 1861, Tennessee initially resisted secession. After the firing on Fort Sumter, Governor Isham G. Harris actively pushed the Volunteer State to stand with the South. Tennessee seceded in May 1861 after a statewide referendum and was admitted to the Confederacy. However, the mountain counties of East Tennessee remained staunchly pro-Union and restive. Kentucky found itself torn between a pro-Union legislature and a pro-secession governor. A compromise declared Kentucky neutral, effectively creating a buffer zone between the Union and the Confederacy stretching from the Appalachian Mountains to the Mississippi River. Union armies gathered north of the Ohio River, while in Tennessee Confederate forces coalesced around Nashville and northern border cities. Several Tennessee units went to Virginia and participated in the war's first major engagement, at Manassas on July 21, 1861. Tension rose during the summer of 1861 as each side waited for the other to tip the balance.

The stalemate in the West was upset in early September 1861 when a Confederate force under Major General Leonidas Polk moved into

Kentucky and captured the town of Columbus on the Mississippi River. This act, spurred by erroneous reports of Federal troops in Paducah, set in motion a race for the state as both sides moved to seize territory. The Kentucky General Assembly in Frankfort voted to remain loyal to the United States, while in late October a separate convention in Russellville created a provisional government and passed an ordinance of secession. Kentucky was admitted into the Confederate States of America. The onset of winter found the Confederates in possession of the southern third of the state, while the rest had fallen into Union hands.

Leonidas Polk. *Perryville Battlefield State Historic Site.*

Both sides spent the winter consolidating their positions and preparing for a major campaign in 1862. Confederate forces, now commanded by General Albert Sidney Johnston, set up a thin defensive line across southern Kentucky. One of the major weaknesses of Johnston's position was that the Tennessee and Cumberland Rivers led southward through his defenses; any determined thrust by Federal troops along those waterways could unhinge his whole line.

Buell's army tested the Confederate position in January, smashing the eastern flank in the Battle of Mill Springs, near Somerset, Kentucky. Grant's force at Paducah next moved south into Tennessee and, in February, captured Forts Henry and Donelson along with sixteen thousand men. At a stroke, Johnston's army in Kentucky was outflanked and its lines of communication to Nashville threatened with rupture. Grant moved up the Tennessee River to Pittsburg Landing near the Mississippi border, while Buell surged toward Nashville.[4]

Faced with the prospect of a defeat in detail, Johnston retreated. He abandoned Nashville and decided to concentrate his scattered commands at Corinth, Mississippi, an easy march from Grant's camp. Polk joined him in Corinth, as did reinforcements under Braxton Bragg from Pensacola. At dawn on April 6, Johnston attacked Grant at Pittsburg Landing. The battle

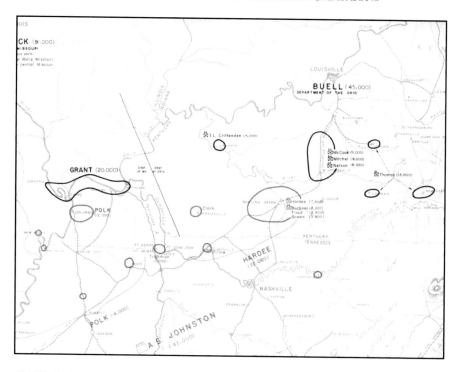

The War in the West, January 1862. From *West Point Atlas of American Wars. Author's collection.*

lasted all day and came excruciatingly close to driving Grant's army into the river, but at the cost of Johnston's life. Much of Buell's army arrived that evening and crossed the river, making good Grant's losses from the day's fighting. The combined Federal forces counterattacked the next day and drove the Confederates (now under General P.G.T. Beauregard) from the field in disorder. Thus ended the Battle of Pittsburg Landing, or Shiloh as the Confederates called it—the first great battle of the Civil War.[5]

After Shiloh, both sides reorganized. Beauregard licked his wounds in Corinth, while the Federal armies prepared to follow up their victory. Major General Henry W. Halleck, the Federal supreme commander in the West, came to Pittsburg Landing and assumed command of both Grant's and Buell's armies. In late April, Halleck's force, now numbering 100,000 men, moved south on a methodical advance toward Corinth. The Union troops averaged one mile of progress per day and, after a month, arrived at Corinth to find it deserted. Beauregard had retreated south to Tupelo without a fight.

Instead of pursuing his enemy to destruction, Halleck divided his forces in an effort to capture territory. In June, Grant's army shifted west and

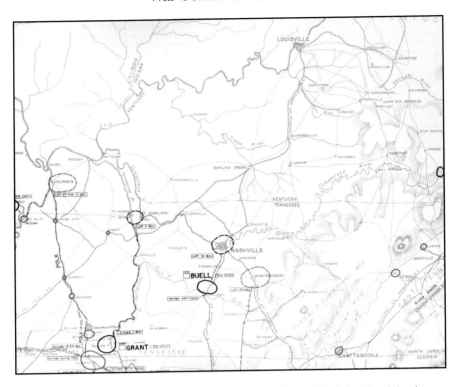

The Western Theater on the eve of the Battle of Shiloh. From *West Point Atlas of American Wars. Author's collection.*

northwest to secure Memphis and West Tennessee, while Buell's Army of the Ohio was ordered eastward from Corinth toward the critical rail junction of Chattanooga. If Buell captured that city, he would hold the gateway to the Deep South and be just one hundred miles from Atlanta. He would also be in position to liberate East Tennessee, a cherished objective for President Abraham Lincoln.[6]

Grant met with swift success in West Tennessee, but Buell's movement progressed slowly due to supply problems. After leaving Corinth in June, the Army of the Ohio made slow progress across northern Mississippi and Alabama toward Chattanooga. Low water in the Tennessee River prevented supply by the navy, forcing Buell's fifty thousand men to depend on the railroads running south and southeast from Nashville for sustenance. The Nashville and Chattanooga Railroad, which was the direct link between its namesake cities, had been laid waste. Instead, the Federals had to depend on the east–west Memphis and Chattanooga Railroad that was easily cut by Confederate marauders. The enemy had also destroyed much of its infrastructure and rolling stock, including two large bridges over the Tennessee River. The Army of the Ohio was forced to rebuild as it marched in the heat of a Mississippi and Alabama summer. Confederate cavalry raids and guerrillas cut the rail lines and harried the army on its advance every step of the way. Southern bandits even murdered a general, Brigadier General Robert McCook, in July. The Army of the Ohio spent much of this edgy summer on half-rations.

In the face of his men's hardship, Buell forbade foraging. This order provoked much resentment in the army, and the men resorted to plundering anyway. A drought had taken its toll on local farms, and many forage parties often failed to find provisions. This rising frustration among the Federal soldiers led to reprisals against Confederate sympathizers, which in turn brought sharp rebukes from Buell's headquarters.[7] Although a small detachment of Buell's army shelled Chattanooga in the middle of July, his main body was only just approaching the city by the end of the month. It had taken his men six weeks to travel from Corinth to the Cumberland Plateau.[8]

As Buell's Federals finally approached their objective, they confronted the formidable terrain shielding Chattanooga. Before reaching that town, an army first needed to control the area between Nashville and Murfreesboro, thirty miles to the southeast of the capital. Fifteen miles past Murfreesboro, the terrain steepens and leads into an area known as the Barrens, a flat and

Chattanooga from Lookout Mountain. *National Archives.*

sandy area forty miles wide at the foot of the Cumberland Plateau. Southeast of Decherd, Winchester and Cowan, Buell's troops encountered the steep Cumberland Plateau itself. Very few roads crossed it, and most of them dipped south into Alabama and Georgia before returning to Tennessee just west of Chattanooga. Chattanooga itself sits in a valley surrounded by hills, with Lookout Mountain to the west, the Cumberland Plateau to the northwest and Missionary Ridge to the east. The Tennessee River wound past Lookout Mountain to front the city and go beyond into East Tennessee. Buell needed to concentrate his army before moving into this forbidding terrain.

As July turned into August, the Army of the Ohio remained strung out on the roads and railroads leading toward Chattanooga. Two divisions under Major Generals Alexander M. McCook and Thomas L. Crittenden stood twelve miles southwest of Chattanooga at Stevenson, Alabama. Several other components of the army stretched westward along the railroad toward Athens, Alabama. Still a third part of the army ranged between Murfreesboro and the Cumberland Plateau in a vain attempt to halt Confederate cavalry raids. This last area was a running sore of casualties for Buell as Confederate horsemen captured numerous detachments, including a major part of the Army of the Ohio's cavalry. Word of Confederate reinforcements in Chattanooga caused Buell to begin concentrating near Decherd to await developments.[9]

In Chattanooga itself, the Confederates had not been idle. Beauregard's force, styled the Army of the Mississippi and numbering some thirty thousand men, was shifting via rail to block and strike the Federals, while Confederates in East Tennessee prepared to operate in concert. The army also brought a new commander; Beauregard had taken ill in June and was replaced by General Braxton Bragg. The entire army had arrived by the end of August.

On July 31, the two primary commanders in Tennessee, General Braxton Bragg and Major General Edmund Kirby Smith, met in Chattanooga to plan a counteroffensive. Kirby Smith had traveled down from Knoxville to meet his counterpart, a man he later described to his wife as "a grim old fellow, but a true soldier." General Bragg hailed from a North Carolina family of social outcasts; some question exists as to whether he was born while his mother was in jail or shortly after she completed her sentence. Bragg's father pushed him into a military career, so the future general graduated from West Point in 1837 and spent the next eighteen years in the U.S. Army, seeing action against the Seminoles in Florida and in the war with Mexico. His achievements at the Battle of Buena Vista in 1847 made him a national hero despite notable blots on his record that included two court-martials, an attempted assassination attempt by his subordinates and

Braxton Bragg. *Library of Congress.*

Edmund Kirby Smith. *Perryville Battlefield State Historic Site.*

a reputation for extreme contentiousness. In the late 1840s, he married and settled in Louisiana. Bragg cast his lot with the Confederacy in 1861 and by 1862 was known as a tough drillmaster but a solid subordinate officer. He had commanded the Army of the Mississippi for only six weeks before this meeting with Kirby Smith.[10]

Both men agreed on a counteroffensive but disagreed initially on the objective. At that point, Nashville was the only Confederate capital city in Union hands, and Bragg wanted to recapture it. As a necessary preliminary operation, Kirby Smith needed to reduce Brigadier General George W. Morgan's seven-thousand-man Federal garrison at Cumberland Gap, on the verge of invading East Tennessee. As both generals further evaluated their options, an invasion of Kentucky seemed to offer brighter prospects. After much deliberation, both men decided to strike northward into Kentucky; Kirby Smith would aim for Lexington and the central Bluegrass, while Bragg would advance through the mountains toward the vital railroad linking Louisville and Nashville. Promises of recruits and forage also attracted them to the Bluegrass State, plus the prospect of maneuvering the Federals out of much of their gains of early 1862. Confederate president Jefferson Davis assented to the plan but left both Bragg and Kirby Smith as independent commanders.

On August 15, Kirby Smith's twenty-one-thousand-man force, redesignated the Army of Kentucky, left Knoxville and marched north toward Kentucky. The war in the West was about to take an important turn.[11]

Chapter 2

Kentucky Round Trip

The Confederate expedition into the Bluegrass State lasted from the middle of August until the end of October 1862. The repercussions of its failure affected operations in the West for the rest of 1862 and well into 1863. Much of what followed sprang directly from the ten weeks in Kentucky.[12]

The Confederate invasion started well as Kirby Smith's army surged into the state and surrounded George Morgan's Federal garrison at Cumberland Gap on August 20. Leaving a nine-thousand-man division under Major General Carter L. Stevenson to watch Morgan's Federals, the rest of Kirby Smith's army moved north to Barbourville along the Old Wilderness Road. The Central Bluegrass stood open for conquest.

Kirby Smith's appearance in Kentucky electrified the North. His presence in Barbourville meant that the largest Union force in the state east of the Tennessee River was now cut off in Cumberland Gap. Brigadier General Jeremiah Boyle, the state's military commander, frantically appealed to higher authorities once Confederate intentions became clear. Reinforcements, mostly new recruits only just mustered into service, streamed south from Indiana and Ohio. General Halleck, now general in chief in Washington, realized the danger and reorganized the Federal command structure by placing Major General Horatio Wright in command over a reorganized Department of the Ohio. By the twenty-third, a Federal force of eight thousand men (known also as the Army of Kentucky) had begun to coalesce at Lexington.

In response to Boyle's pleas for help, Buell detached several generals and sent them north to help organize the defense of Kentucky. The highest-ranking of them was Major General William Nelson. A Kentucky native, Nelson had served as an officer in the U.S. Navy before the war. He was a very large man who weighed more than three hundred pounds and was known as "Bull" because of his direct and aggressive temperament. In 1861, he had recruited and trained some of the first Kentucky Federal units and later commanded a division at Shiloh with some success. Nelson brought two of his subordinates with him: Brigadier Generals Charles Cruft and Mahlon Manson. After organizing his command, Nelson pushed his men forward to Richmond to scout and await developments. The Confederates did not make him wait long.

Kirby Smith moved north and met the Federal pickets six miles south of Richmond late on August 29. By chance, Nelson was away

Carter Stevenson. *Perryville Battlefield State Historic Site.*

from his army, so Manson commanded in his stead. Thinking that he was facing only cavalry, Manson sent half of his force south from Richmond on the steamy morning of August 30. They collided with the Confederates near the Rogersville crossroads, a few miles outside of town. Brigadier General Patrick Cleburne's Confederate division led the advance, and his men soon stalemated the Federals along a row of hills south of Rogersville. Outnumbered, he called for reinforcements before suffering a severe facial wound that rendered him temporarily unable to speak. Kirby Smith took command personally and directed his forces to envelop the Federals via a draw that led past their western flank. The attack got underway at 10:00 a.m., causing the rookie Federal units to waver and collapse under the Confederate pressure. The survivors streamed northward toward Richmond.

Manson managed to rally his command at the Rogersville crossroads and made a stand there at noon. Fighting the Confederates on even terms, they held their own for about an hour until a failed attack by Cruft's brigade broke the stalemate. Kirby Smith's men lunged forward, and the entire Federal line collapsed again in rout. General Nelson arrived on the field as the dazed survivors poured into Richmond itself. The Bull managed to collect about 2,200 men for a last stand outside the town.

Kirby Smith's veterans arrived opposite Nelson's position at about 4:00 p.m. They had been marching and fighting for ten hours in oppressive heat and drought but sensed victory. The Confederates quickly deployed and advanced. "Our troops stood about three volleys" before breaking, recalled Nelson. As he tried to rally his men, General Nelson suffered a serious wound and was carried off the field. All further Federal organization dissolved as the Union Army of Kentucky fled northward. Most of the fugitives were swept into the arms of Confederate cavalry along the northern edges of Richmond; Generals Nelson and Cruft, plus two thousand of their men, managed to escape to the northeast. In one day, Kirby Smith had destroyed the only significant Federal force in the Central Bluegrass.

The Battle of Richmond ranks as arguably the most complete Confederate victory of the Civil War. Nelson's army lost 4,300 prisoners, plus 1,050 killed and wounded, out of 7,000 men. Kirby Smith also engaged about 7,000 men but lost a mere 624 to all causes. Considering that this battle occurred the same day that General Robert E. Lee drove a large Federal army at Manassas off the field in rout, August 30, 1862, has to rank as one of the best days of the Confederacy's life.

Kirby Smith paused on the thirty-first to replenish supplies and parole prisoners and then started for Lexington. The Confederate Army of Kentucky entered the city on September 2 to a thunderous reception. One of the Confederates remembered that "the balconies, house tops, and windows in fact every place available for view was filled with people cheering and waving handkerchiefs while we marched through the streets." Not resting on his laurels, Kirby Smith sent his cavalry west toward Louisville. Other detachments probed north toward Cincinnati. Frankfort fell on September 4, becoming the only capital of a loyal state captured by the Confederacy during the war.

On September 6, Kirby Smith wrote to President Davis to summarize his campaign so far. He especially noted "the enthusiasm of the people here on the entry of our troops. They evidently regarded us as their deliverers from oppression and have continued in every way to prove to us that the heart of Kentucky is with the South in this struggle." Amid all the approbation, Kirby Smith did discern a threat to his gains from the Army of the Ohio: "If Bragg occupies Buell we can have nothing to oppose us [in Kentucky] but raw levies, and by the blessing of God will always dispose of them as we did on the memorable August 30."

While Kirby Smith advanced into the Bluegrass, Bragg remained at Chattanooga refitting his thirty thousand men for the coming campaign. He wrote to President Davis denouncing most of his officers for incompetence

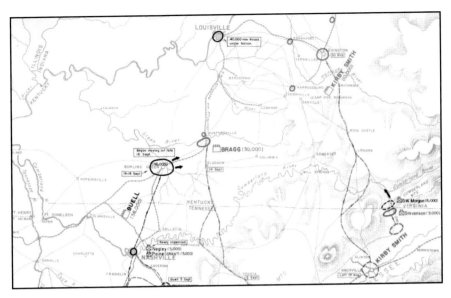

The Kentucky Campaign through the fall of Munfordville on September 17, 1862. From *West Point Atlas of American Wars. Author's collection.*

and unsuccessfully requested sweeping powers to arrange his subordinate commanders as he saw fit. Bragg also made it clear to everyone that he mistrusted most of his senior subordinates and their abilities. These attitudes did little but poison the command climate of the Army of the Mississippi.

The Army of the Mississippi moved out of Chattanooga on August 28, two days before Kirby Smith's victory at Richmond. Bragg's columns wound northward though the Cumberland Plateau and arrived at Sparta, Tennessee, on September 6. Buell reacted slowly to this movement, initially favoring to fight near Sparta but instead ordering his army back to Nashville. By September 6, much of the Army of the Ohio was in that city or nearby. Reinforcements from Grant's army brought Buell's strength to about fifty-five thousand men.

Entering Kentucky near Glasgow, Bragg's army groped northwest toward the strategic Louisville & Nashville (L&N) Railroad, Buell's lifeline between his major supply base at Louisville and forward depot at Nashville. On September 14, a Confederate brigade suffered a rough repulse by the four-thousand-man Federal garrison at Munfordville, where the railroad crossed the Green River. Bragg responded by besieging the garrison, calling for its surrender on the evening of September 16. Munfordville's commander, Colonel John T. Wilder, after some deliberation and a visit to Confederate lines, handed over his command at 4:00 a.m. on September 17. A jubilant Bragg celebrated his first victory as army commander.

The capitulation at Munfordville ranks as one of the largest surrenders of U.S. troops in the Civil War. As Wilder's men vacated the post on parole, several hundred miles to the east the Army of the Potomac and Army of Northern Virginia fought the Battle of Antietam, which resulted in nearly twenty-four thousand casualties. September 17, 1862, is the bloodiest single day in American history, with about twenty-eight thousand men killed, wounded, missing or captured in that twenty-four-hour period.

That same day, George Morgan abandoned Cumberland Gap and commenced a sixteen-day cat-and-mouse hunt in the mountains of eastern Kentucky as he sought to escape to Ohio. Battling drought, dwindling rations and Confederate cavalry under Colonel John Hunt Morgan, his men covered 219 miles to the Ohio River, escaping on October 3 virtually without loss.

Meanwhile, Buell regrouped at Bowling Green and cautiously maneuvered toward Munfordville. Bragg's army stood in a fantastic tactical situation, but logistically it was in serious trouble. Both men and animals suffered for want of water in the worsening drought. The Federal garrison at Munfordville, in place since the previous December, had picked the local area clean of forage. The Army of the Mississippi's quartermasters reported to General Bragg that if they stayed in Munfordville more than a few days, the army would begin to starve. Judging himself too weak to attack Buell, and without supplies to stay in place, Bragg was forced to move. Accordingly, on September 20, Bragg abandoned Munfordville and turned northeast toward Bardstown, where he expected to resupply and unite with Kirby Smith's army. Buell's road to Louisville was open. The Army of the Ohio hustled northward toward Kentucky's largest city, reaching it on September 25.

The Army of Mississippi camped around Bardstown in good spirits, although many men in the ranks expressed frustration over the abandonment of Munfordville. Far more frustrating was the decided reluctance of male Kentuckians to join the Confederate army. Bragg had brought fifteen thousand rifles with him into Kentucky and expected to find plenty of demand for them. Unfortunately, the anticipated wave of recruits did not materialize. Despite statewide recruiting appeals, the Confederates succeeded in raising only about 1,500 soldiers. Efforts to boost recruiting by transferring favorite sons John C. Breckinridge and the Orphan Brigade soldiers to Kentucky from Louisiana ran afoul of delays. In the end, only about 5,000 Kentuckians joined the Confederate army, and most of those went into the cavalry.

This lack of enthusiasm did not go unnoticed in the Confederate ranks. Kirby Smith lamented that Kentuckians' "hearts are evidently with us, but their blue-grass and fat-grass [cattle] are against us." There was something to this theory, as the Union authorities had issued several decrees that ensured that pro-Confederates who fought placed their property at risk of confiscation. With sizeable Federal forces in and around Louisville, many in the state realized that the campaign had only just begun. Bragg and Kirby Smith needed to assure the populace that the Confederacy was there to stay.

John C. Breckinridge. *National Archives.*

Bragg's mood darkened as he realized how hesitant Kentucky recruits were proving to be. People around army headquarters began to notice that the general was developing an increasing disdain for all things Kentucky. Bragg's frustration came through in a dispatch to the Confederate War Department on September 25:

> *I regret to say we are sadly disappointed at the want of action by our friends in Kentucky. We have so far received no accession to this army. General Smith has secured about a brigade—not half our losses by casualties of different kinds. We have 15,000 stand of arms and no one to use them. Unless a change occurs soon we must abandon the garden spot of Kentucky to its cupidity. The love of ease and fear of pecuniary loss are the fruitful sources of this evil. Kentucky and Tennessee are redeemed if we can be supported, but at least 50,000 men will be necessary, and a few weeks will decide the question. Should we have to retire, much in the way of supplies and morale will be lost, and the redemption of Kentucky will be indefinitely postponed, if not rendered impossible.*

The Confederates now controlled virtually all of Kentucky east of the Louisville & Nashville Railroad. Thinking that Buell would need weeks to refit, Bragg went on the defensive.

Meanwhile, in Louisville, the Federals energetically prepared to reverse the situation. Buell's frustrated men had retired three hundred miles without a major battle, and that fact stung their pride. Unlike their comrades in the East, the announcement of Lincoln's preliminary Emancipation Proclamation on September 22 excited little comment from Buell's soldiers. Reinforcements and new recruits brought the Army of the Ohio's strength to seventy-five thousand men. Buell prepared to advance from Louisville into the Central Bluegrass while feinting toward Frankfort, thus forcing the Confederates to fight or retreat to Tennessee.

General Buell's stock was at a nadir, and some of his subordinates pushed openly for a command change. In Washington, the War Department had also decided that a new commander was necessary. General in Chief Halleck sent a courier westward with orders relieving Buell and replacing him with Major General George H. Thomas, a respected and experienced Virginian who had remained loyal to the Union. The orders were not to take effect "if General Buell should be found in the presence of the enemy preparing to fight a battle." The relief directive arrived on the twenty-ninth, finding Buell's army in the midst of organizing, supplying and planning for a major campaign into Central Kentucky.[13]

When he received the dispatch, Buell immediately moved to turn over command. The problem was that Thomas refused to take it. As the Virginian wrote to Halleck, "General Buell's preparations have been completed to move against the enemy, and I therefore respectfully ask that he may be retained in command. My position is very embarrassing, not being as well informed as I should be as the commander of this army and on the assumption of such a responsibility." Exasperated but unwilling to referee, Halleck informed both men that the orders were "suspended" and confirmed that General Buell retained command. Yet Buell still had the prospect of relief hanging over him at any moment.

Buell managed to keep his job on September 29, but that day he did lose an experienced subordinate. Bull Nelson had recovered from his Richmond wound and was back on duty when the Army of the Ohio arrived in Louisville. His experiences at Richmond had given him a poor impression of Indiana troops, and General Nelson made no secret of his dislike of Hoosiers. This attitude bristled on Brigadier General Jefferson C. Davis, a prickly Indianan who took great pride in his state. The two men got into a shouting match, and Nelson sent him to Cincinnati under arrest on the twenty-fifth. General Wright released him from arrest and ordered him back to Louisville and the Army of the Ohio. Davis returned with Governor Levi Morton of Indiana, who happened to be going there on an inspection trip.

At about 7:30 a.m. on the morning of the twenty-ninth, Davis, Morton and several aides ran into Nelson in the lobby of the Galt House hotel in downtown Louisville. The two generals exchanged words, and Nelson slapped Davis. As the Bull walked away, an enraged Davis grabbed a pistol from an aide and followed Nelson upstairs. After some more words, Davis shot Nelson in the chest. The Bull collapsed and died an hour later, and Davis was placed under arrest.

Later that day, General Buell announced his command structure for the upcoming campaign. For the first time in its history the Army of the Ohio would contain corps, numbered I, II and III. Each corps contained about twenty-five thousand men and brought infantry, artillery and cavalry under a single commander. They were commanded by Major Generals Alexander McCook, Thomas L. Crittenden and Charles C. Gilbert, respectively. Thomas, whom Buell now viewed as a threat, was elevated to the sinecure of second in command of the army. The reorganized Army of the Ohio left Louisville on October 1. A force of twenty thousand moved toward Frankfort, while Buell's main body of fifty-five thousand men aimed for Bardstown.

Meanwhile, Bragg had left Bardstown and was preparing to install the Confederate state government at Frankfort. Buell's advance caught him off guard, and he vainly tried to direct the Confederate forces to counterattack the Federal advance. General Polk, in command at Bardstown, on his own initiative abandoned the town and retreated eastward. Bragg concurred with the decision and tried to concentrate the Confederate forces near Harrodsburg, forty miles southwest of Lexington. The Federals ran part of his army to ground at Perryville, ten miles southwest of Harrodsburg, on the night of October 7.

Believing that Buell's main body was at Frankfort, Bragg ordered Polk to attack the Federal force outside Perryville the next morning, October 8. Polk realized that he faced the bulk of the Federal army and stayed on the defensive. Angry at this disobedience, Bragg rode to Perryville and ordered an attack against McCook's I Corps for that afternoon. His command of sixteen thousand men would attack in echelon from north to south, hoping to break and rout McCook's line.

The Confederate offensive began as planned at 2:00 p.m. Fighting initially swirled around Lieutenant Charles Parsons's eight-gun battery atop Open Knob before that position fell to the Confederates. Other troops swung into action, and by 4:15 p.m., McCook's entire line was in retreat toward the key

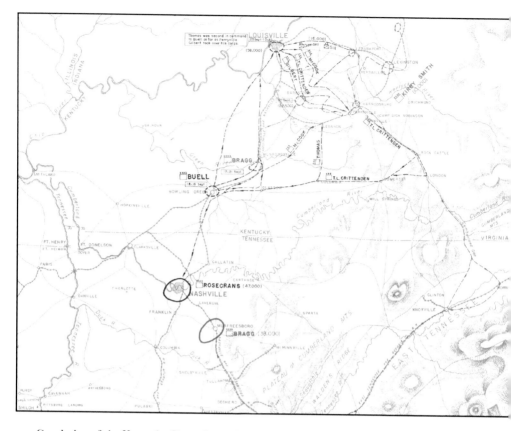

Conclusion of the Kentucky Campaign and the armies' return to Tennessee, October and November 1862. From *West Point Atlas of American Wars. Author's collection.*

Dixville Crossroads, the possession of which would determine whether I Corps would be destroyed.

As the sun began to set, belated Federal reinforcements arrived and combined with McCook's battered corps to blunt the Confederate momentum in savage fighting within yards of the Dixville Crossroads. At dusk, General Polk was almost captured while reconnoitering. The battle also spread to Perryville itself, resulting in the first major street fighting of the Civil War. Darkness ended the engagement; after five hours of combat, 7,500 men lay killed or wounded or went missing. The Battle of Perryville was the largest and bloodiest battle ever fought in Kentucky.

That night, Bragg finally appreciated the true situation and pulled back to Harrodsburg. Buell pursued but also sent a force under Thomas and Crittenden to cut the Confederate road to Tennessee. Bragg abandoned Harrodsburg and retired southeast to Camp Breckinridge, a former training base that now served as his major supply depot. There he decided to make a stand and try to salvage the campaign. Buell's army followed at a measured pace.

As he sat among his supplies, gloom set in as Bragg recalled the failed recruiting efforts and how the bright prospects of the Kentucky Campaign had gone glimmering. On October 12, he sent an update to Richmond and gave vent to his frustration at the end of the message:

> *The campaign here was predicated on a belief and the most positive assurances that the people of this country would rise in mass to assert their independence. No people ever had so favorable an opportunity, but I am distressed to add there is little or no disposition to avail of it. Willing perhaps to accept their independence, they are neither disposed nor willing to risk their lives or their property in its achievement. With ample means to arm 20,000 men and a force with that to fully redeem the State we have not yet issued half the arms left us by casualties incident to the campaign.*

General Bragg had lost heart for the campaign and was looking for a way out.

As it had throughout the Kentucky operation, the supply factor again disturbed Bragg's mind at Camp Breckinridge. First, the camp was found to have little more than four days' rations for the entire Confederate force of forty-five thousand men. They could not withstand a siege or a major battle. Also at this point, the dry weather began to turn, and autumn rains started. It would not be long before weather effectively closed the Wilderness Road over Cumberland Gap for the winter. Both of these factors forced an immediate decision whether to stay in Kentucky or retire southward.

On October 13, Bragg decided to head for Tennessee. That day, the Confederates pulled out of Camp Breckinridge and marched for Cumberland Gap and Knoxville. Anything they could not carry was destroyed. Buell's army methodically pursued, and Federal cavalry repeatedly clashed with Bragg's horsemen. Terrain and bushwhackers also created problems for Bragg's soldiers, but by October 24, much of the army crossed through Cumberland Gap back into Tennessee. The remainder followed within a few days, and by October 31, the Confederates had abandoned the Bluegrass State.

The decision to leave Kentucky was heartbreaking for Confederate Kentuckians. John Hunt Morgan remained with his cavalry at Lexington and, on October 17, fought a small battle a mile outside of town in a futile effort to prevent Federal reoccupation of his hometown. Perhaps the saddest Kentuckians were Breckinridge's Orphan Brigade soldiers, who were finally on their way to join Bragg in mid-October. They had not been anywhere near home since the previous February, and each day the anticipation grew as they marched north from Knoxville. When the Orphans camped on October 16, the mountains of Kentucky were in view. The next morning, the men formed up in full expectation of camping the following night in their home state. But just before the march began, a courier delivered orders to Breckinridge ordering them to back to Knoxville. Bragg's decision to end the campaign had made their move northward unnecessary.[14]

Buell's troops pursued Bragg to just south of London and then broke off on October 19 and marched west toward the L&N Railroad. General Buell's leisurely operations after Perryville had generated the ire of Washington, and by late October, General Halleck was again looking for a new commander. Dissatisfaction with Buell had also grown within the Army of the Ohio's officer corps and threatened to spill into the open. On October 24, Buell was replaced with Major General William S. Rosecrans. Before the year ended, Buell would face a court of inquiry about the campaign that issued mixed findings but preferred no charges. Rosecrans departed from his post in Mississippi to take command of the army, which was also renamed formally the XIV Corps, informally the Army of the Cumberland.[15]

Perryville ended the last serious Confederate attempt to turn Kentucky to the Confederate cause. The scene of war now shifted southward, and both sides prepared to meet again in the Volunteer State. Although physically the armies left the Bluegrass State behind, the Kentucky Campaign would cast a shadow over the subsequent Middle Tennessee operations.

Chapter 3

Rosecrans Advances

William Starke Rosecrans joined his new command at Bowling Green on November 1. An Ohio native, Rosecrans graduated from West Point ranked fifth in the class of 1842. Because of his high class standing, he became an engineer officer and spent much of his army career building, renovating and expanding fortifications along the East Coast. He resigned his commission in 1854, going into the canal and mining business in western Virginia for a time. Rosecrans later founded a kerosene lamp company, but it failed after he was injured in an industrial accident and his partners could not carry on without him. Rejoining the U.S. Army at the Civil War's outbreak, Rosecrans in 1861 served as aide, principal deputy and successor to General McClellan in West Virginia; in the spring of 1862, he was transferred to Halleck's army before Corinth. In early October, he fought and won the Battle of Corinth, thus securing Union control of northern Mississippi and western Tennessee. A gregarious person with a sharp mind and eye for detail, General Rosecrans was a rising star in the fall of 1862.[16]

As soon as he assumed command, Rosecrans faced a personnel problem involving General Thomas, Buell's second in command at Perryville and a man esteemed throughout the Army of the Cumberland. Because of the situation with Buell in Louisville and the suspension of his appointment orders, Thomas felt that he should have received command of the army instead of Rosecrans. By date of rank, Thomas was the army's senior officer. A "deeply mortified and aggrieved" Thomas wrote to Halleck in protest and received a reply that Rosecrans's commission had been backdated to March 21, 1862. That settled the matter for the Virginian: "I have no objection whatever to serving under General Rosecrans, now that I know his

William S. Rosecrans, seen in 1861 as a brigadier general. *National Archives.*

George Thomas. *Perryville Battlefield State Historic Site.*

commission dates prior to mine." To help soothe his subordinate's feelings, Rosecrans offered Thomas his choice of taking a corps command or being the army's second in command; Thomas selected the corps.[17]

The soldiers themselves were curious about their new commander. In contrast to the remote Buell, Rosecrans soon established himself as a visible and active presence among the men. "The army as a whole did not manifest much regret at the change of commanders," wrote Brigadier General Philip H. Sheridan, a sentiment that many veterans echoed in their letters and memoirs. Some officers bristled at the new commander's profanity and vocal Catholicism, but he made a good overall impression.[18]

After regrouping for a few days, Rosecrans marched his army south to Nashville. His lead elements arrived in the Tennessee capital on November 7, and the rest straggled in over the next eleven days. This influx of soldiers transformed Nashville. "The whole country around the city, on both sides of the [Cumberland] river, is one tented field, over whose vast surface scores of thousands of cheerful campfires gleam by night, while, by day they envelop the sky in a pall of smoke," noted the *Nashville Daily Union*.[19]

Nashville as it appeared from the steps of the Tennessee state capitol in 1864. *National Archives.*

As the Army of the Cumberland returned to Tennessee, so did its nemesis. The Confederates marched via Cumberland Gap to Knoxville and then traveled by train to Chattanooga. Wanting to threaten Nashville and possibly attack the city, Bragg directed his troops to Tullahoma and Murfreesboro, where they arrived starting November 12. His men had been marching and fighting continuously since October 2 and were worn out. Bragg decided to halt and refit, deploying his men northwest and west of Murfreesboro. On November 20, his force of forty-five thousand men officially became known as the Army of Tennessee.[20]

The round trip to Kentucky had produced supplies, some recruits and provender that would sustain the army into 1863, but the overall objective of the campaign proved elusive. General Bragg's sometimes unsteady conduct of the operation caused controversy, which spilled into the open as the army crossed the state line. The campaign's failure soured Bragg on Kentuckians, a feeling that he did not conceal and one that was warmly returned by his Kentucky-born subordinates. Polk, Hardee and Kirby Smith all evinced a loss of confidence in Bragg; Polk and Kirby Smith made their views known to friends in the Confederate government. Jefferson Davis called Bragg to Richmond to account for the withdrawal from Kentucky and sent summonses to Polk and Kirby Smith. The two men aired their grievances of how Bragg's erratic leadership and scattering of forces had dissipated the Confederate invasion and ultimately wrecked the campaign. In the end, Davis sustained Bragg based on his administrative merits, lack of a good replacement and a feeling that the general needed another try. After returning to Tennessee, Bragg healed the breach with Kirby Smith; Polk and Hardee proved harder to convince. Significantly, many of the division and brigade commanders remained pro-Bragg, or at least neutral, at this point. Nonetheless, dangerous cracks had opened in the Army of Tennessee's high command.[21]

Bragg's army retained essentially the same organization it brought out of Kentucky, although some shuffling of units occurred as weak regiments and brigades were consolidated. It was divided into three infantry corps of roughly equal size, each named after its commander. One corps went to Lieutenant General Leonidas Polk, the same man whose move to Columbus a year earlier had done so much to unsettle the Western Theater. Polk was a West Point graduate but had immediately resigned from the army and had spent the last thirty-five years as an Episcopal bishop in Louisiana. He was closely connected to Confederate President Jefferson Davis and owed his high rank to Davis's patronage more than any demonstrated ability. General Polk "possessed all the requisites of a great soldier, except strategy and tactical combination," wrote a subordinate. By date of rank, the bishop was the senior corps commander in the army. Polk's Corps contained two divisions led by two major generals: the competent Alabamian Jones Withers and Benjamin F. Cheatham, a hard-drinking and profane former militiaman from Nashville.[22]

Bragg's second corps was led by the highly capable Lieutenant General William Hardee of Georgia. Hardee was one of the best-known generals on either side because he had authored a tactics manual adopted by both the Union and Confederate armies. He was a former commandant of cadets at West Point, and many high-ranking officers on both sides knew and respected his military mind. Hardee's Corps contained two divisions, both commanded by Kentuckians. One was a crack outfit under Major General Simon Bolivar Buckner, the man had who surrendered Fort Donelson the previous February. The other division was led by Major General John C. Breckinridge, the former vice president of the United States under James Buchanan and a leading Kentucky-born Confederate. His division had been cobbled together by combining troops from the Gulf Coast with elements of a division disbanded after command failures in the Kentucky campaign.[23]

Kirby Smith's former Army of Kentucky made up the third corps in Bragg's army. His two veteran divisions were directed by Tennessean Major General John P. McCown, a prickly officer who had been left behind to command restive East Tennessee during the Kentucky Campaign, and Virginian Major General Carter L. Stevenson, who had acquitted himself well in Kentucky. A cavalry division under Brigadier General Joseph Wheeler rounded out the Army of Tennessee.[24]

William Hardee. *Perryville Battlefield State Historic Site.*

As Bragg refit around Murfreesboro, President Davis reorganized the Confederate high command in the West. On November 24, 1862, he consolidated all Confederate forces between the Mississippi River and the Appalachian Mountains into a single department. General Joseph E. Johnston, just recovered from serious wounds sustained the previous May in Virginia, took charge of this large area. A formal man who was respected among his peers and subordinates, his relations with Richmond had proven to be frosty in the past. Upon arriving in Chattanooga, Johnston saw that he had much responsibility but little power; his key subordinates were authorized to communicate directly with Richmond instead of going through him as their superior.[25]

Meanwhile, in Nashville, General Rosecrans settled into his new headquarters at the George W. Cunningham House at 13 High Street.[26] He set about addressing the three major problems that confronted him before undertaking a new campaign. The first problem concerned the deplorable condition of his army. Many of his soldiers had worn out their uniforms and equipment, while others had not been paid in months. The army's staff and medical services had atrophied due to Buell's neglect. Some infantry regiments were equipped with substandard weapons, while the army's cavalry had never recovered from the exertions and losses of the summer and early fall. Rosecrans worked with a will to address these deficiencies. He requested $1 million from Washington to address the back pay issue, weeded out incompetent staff and medical officers and reequipped his men as best he could. Rosecrans created a Pioneer Brigade of 1,700 men to meet the army's engineering requirements on campaign. "We must have cavalry, and cavalry arms, and a capable division commander," he wrote to Halleck; soon Brigadier General David S. Stanley arrived from Rosecrans's old Mississippi command to take charge of the mounted arm. As November turned into December, the army gained a new combat edge.[27]

Rosecrans's second problem concerned his supply line. This critical issue drove all other considerations and exerted constant pressure on the Army of the Cumberland's operations. Throughout the war, of the three major Federal armies (the Army of the Potomac, Army of the Cumberland and the Army of the Tennessee), the Army of the Cumberland consistently had the longest and most vulnerable supply lines. Rosecrans's main logistical base was at Louisville, 183 miles north of his forward depot at Nashville. Two viable supply routes connected the cities: via ship along the Ohio and Cumberland Rivers or along the Louisville & Nashville (L&N) Railroad. Low water levels at the Harpeth Shoals, 20 miles downstream of Nashville, limited river traffic that fall to all but the shallowest-draft ships, forcing Rosecrans's lifeline to ride the rails of the L&N.

The L&N ran south from Louisville up Muldraugh Hill (site of present-day Fort Knox) and then through Elizabethtown and south to the Green River crossing at Munfordville, site of the siege and surrender in September 1862. It then headed south to Bowling Green and then southeast into Tennessee, entering the state at Mitchellsville. From there, the railroad ran through an eight-hundred-foot-long tunnel north of Gallatin. After passing the rail yards at Gallatin, it turned southwest and entered Nashville from the north, where it linked with the Nashville & Chattanooga Railroad to service traffic headed southeast. Almost every one of its 183 miles passed through neutral or hostile territory, making the L&N highly vulnerable to raids by Confederate cavalry or guerrillas. Colonel Morgan's cavalry had done serious damage to the line, even burning the Gallatin Tunnel in August. The L&N's tracks were operational to Mitchellsville in the middle of November, which necessitated a long and slow wagon trip over the forty miles from that point to Nashville. The railroad reopened all the way to the state capital on November 25; the arrival of a train from Louisville made the front page of the Nashville newspapers. In the 365-day period from July 1, 1862, to June 30, 1863, the railroad was completely functional only seven months and 12 days. Each closing of the L&N slowed or halted Rosecrans's supply buildup and operations.[28]

The third problem confronting the army involved the external pressures coming from the United States that December. Needing political capital in the wake of reverses in the 1862 midterm elections, and with the Emancipation Proclamation taking effect on January 1, 1863, President Lincoln prodded his forces to make December campaigns and engage in "hard, tough fighting that will hurt somebody." Grant's Army of the Tennessee tried twice that month to take Vicksburg, Mississippi, but failed both times. In Virginia, the Army of the Potomac vainly hurled itself against the heights behind Fredericksburg on December 13, suffering a humiliating defeat that precipitated a cabinet crisis.

In Nashville, Rosecrans continued with his buildup. Halleck prodded him to attack East Tennessee, but Rosecrans begged off because of logistical difficulties. He was more focused on advancing southeast, reasoning that the fall of Chattanooga would force the Confederates out of East Tennessee by default. Rosecrans needed to accumulate supplies in Nashville for the coming campaign and was forced to use some of his troops to guard the L&N. On December 4, Halleck wrote, "The President is very impatient with your long stay in Nashville…Twice I have been asked to designate someone else to command your army. If you remain one more week at Nashville, I cannot prevent your removal." Rosecrans called Halleck's bluff by saying that he was "insensible" to such threats. Nonetheless, the message was clear: Rosecrans needed to fight before the year ended.[29]

Outside the city, the Union and Confederate pickets faced each other in the vicinity of La Vergne. Both sides fought outpost skirmishes almost daily, but in early December the Confederates became more active. On December 1, Bragg ordered Morgan to "operate on the enemy's lines of communications in the rear of Nashville…capture and destroy his trains; burn his bridges, depots, trestle-work, &c. In fine, harass him in every conceivable way in your power." To prevent just such a raid, Rosecrans had scattered several infantry brigades in the key towns east and southeast of Gallatin. As Morgan calculated how to get at the L&N, he realized that the Federal garrison at Hartsville needed to be suppressed, as it controlled the best ford along that part of the Cumberland River. Bragg concurred, and on December 6 Morgan set off with 1,500 infantry and cavalry to capture the place.[30]

John Hunt Morgan. *Perryville Battlefield State Historic Site.*

Confederate intelligence estimated the Hartsville garrison to be less than one thousand men, but in reality more than two thousand Federals of Colonel Absalom B. Moore's 39th Brigade were camped on the heights south of town overlooking the river. Moore had taken command four days earlier of a force composed of the 104th Illinois, the 106th Ohio and 108th Ohio Infantry Regiments, the 2nd Indiana Cavalry and detachments of cavalry and artillery from Kentucky and Indiana. Except for the 2nd Indiana Cavalry, none of Moore's units had been in battle. A strong brigade of four thousand veterans under Colonel John M. Harlan camped nine miles to the west at Castalian Springs. Feeling complacent, Moore neglected to scout or picket along the river.[31]

Morgan's Confederates crossed the Cumberland undetected during the night of December 6–7. His men were moving as dawn broke on Sunday, December 7. Swinging west of Moore's position, Morgan sent some of his cavalry into Hartsville itself to cut off the Federal retreat. The rest of his command approached from the west, while Morgan's two small howitzers woke the Federal camp with fire from south of the river. At about 6:30 a.m., the cavalry encountered Moore's pickets, which raised the general alarm. "I could distinctly see and hear the officers ordering their men to fall in, preparing for resistance," recalled Morgan.[32]

The Cumberland River at Hartsville, as seen in 2011. *Photograph by Terry R. Woodson.*

Caught by surprise, the Federals formed a line in some confusion on a ridge overlooking the river northwest of the Federal camp. The Indiana horsemen screened the north flank, while the three infantry regiments formed a line facing west with the 104th on the left, the 106th in the center and the 108th to the right. "It was at once plain that the force there was much stronger than it had been represented to be," noted Colonel Basil Duke of Morgan's command. Realizing that time was not on his side, Morgan sent two of his dismounted cavalry regiments in a frontal attack against the Federal line, while other infantry and cavalry units hit the Union right. "The battle opened about 7 a.m.," recalled an officer in the 104th Illinois. "When Morgan's advance came within musket range the firing became general and continuous on both sides for some time. Morgan still advanced, but slower." While the 104th Illinois held firm, the Ohioans to its right suffered under Confederate pressure to their front and flanks. Both Ohio regiments soon wavered and broke. Colonel Moore ordered a charge but changed his mind and directed the Federals back to their camps for a new stand. As Morgan's troops closed in, Moore surrendered his entire command after a fight lasting no more than seventy-five minutes.[33]

Hartsville Battlefield in 2011, looking east from the ridge where the Federals made their stand. Colonel Moore's men retreated into the distant lowlands, where they surrendered. *Photograph by Terry R. Woodson.*

An elated Morgan counted his prisoners and realized what he had accomplished. "The result exceeded my own expectation, but still I felt that my position was a most perilous one," he wrote. The Confederates gathered their prisoners and plunder and sent them across the Cumberland at Hart's Ferry, just below Moore's former camp. Morgan's premonition of danger was correct: Colonel Harlan's infantry had heard the firing at 7:30 a.m. and were marching fast toward Hartsville. Brushing aside Confederate scouts and delaying detachments, Harlan's infantry arrived just as Morgan's last elements departed Hart's Ferry. "They were fired upon," Harlan reported, "when they abandoned the wagons and fled precipitately across the river… Pursuit was utterly impracticable."[34]

Morgan's troopers marched south with their prisoners and plunder, arriving in Murfreesboro on the ninth. Against a loss of 139 killed and wounded, Morgan had killed, wounded and captured more than 2,000 enemy soldiers. The prisoners were paroled and sent north. "Deep was the sting of this disaster," recalled an officer of the 104th Illinois. In Washington, President Lincoln was incensed at the news of Moore's defeat.[35]

The Hartsville victory buoyed Confederate spirits, and Bragg confidently predicted that Rosecrans would go into winter quarters in Nashville. A second event brightened the month when, on December 14, newly promoted Brigadier General Morgan wed Mattie Ready in Murfreesboro. General Polk officiated the ceremony, while Morgan's groomsmen included Generals Bragg, Breckinridge, Hardee and Cheatham. A week later, Morgan took his cavalry to raid the L&N in Kentucky.[36]

During this time, the composition of Bragg's army changed. Grant's advances against Vicksburg caused concern, and in consequence President Davis ordered Stevenson's division to Mississippi, reducing Bragg's strength to thirty-seven thousand men. Generals Kirby Smith and Buckner were also transferred away, the former to the Trans-Mississippi and the latter to East Tennessee. Buckner's old division came under the command of Major General Patrick R. Cleburne.[37]

In Nashville, General Rosecrans had been looking for an opening to strike. These detachments gave him the opportunity, and on Christmas Day he called a council of war. The commanding general's exuberant personality shone through as he explained the plan of advance and announced that it would begin in the next day. In case his commanders had not understood his intent, Rosecrans closed by exhorting them to "Press them hard! Drive them out of their nests! Make them fight or run! Fight them! Fight them! Fight I say!" The events of the next week would test those words to the limit.[38]

Chapter 4

Bloody New Year's Eve

The Army of the Cumberland left its Nashville camps at dawn on December 26, 1862. Rosecrans's cavalry and intelligence network gave him a good idea of Confederate dispositions. Bragg had spread his thirty-seven thousand troops in a wide arc, with Polk's Corps, plus Breckinridge's division, around Murfreesboro and the balance of Hardee's Corps twenty miles to the west near Triune and Eagleville. McCown's division camped twelve miles east of Murfreesboro at Readyville. Each of these three elements stood a day's march from help, which rendered the Army of Tennessee subject to defeat in detail.[39]

For the upcoming campaign, Rosecrans divided his army into three corps-sized wings (Left, Center and Right), numbering more than seventy thousand men. Based on Buell's old corps structure, these formations had been reorganized and renumbered during the Nashville interlude. Now this army would face its first major test under its new commander.[40]

Command of the Right Wing went to Major General Alexander McCook of Ohio, one of Rosecrans's most experienced subordinates. General McCook was a flamboyant character known for his appetite, fleshy figure and luxurious lifestyle. He had a good résumé, including a stint as tactics instructor at West Point. The general was one of fourteen in his family to serve in the Union army during the Civil War; his older brother, Robert, had been killed by Confederate raiders a few months before. McCook commanded three divisions under Brigadier Generals Jefferson C. Davis, Richard W. Johnson and Philip Sheridan. All three were experienced commanders, especially Sheridan. Davis and Johnson had each just been released from confinement—Davis for the murder of General Nelson in September and Johnson for his capture by Confederates the previous summer.[41]

Major General Thomas L. Crittenden of Kentucky led Rosecrans's Left Wing. Unlike McCook's pro-Union clan, secession had torn apart this general's family and friends. Crittenden's residence was in Louisville, and he was an old friend of Simon B. Buckner from their service in the Kentucky State Guard. His alcoholic older brother was a major general in the Confederate army and had just resigned his commission in disgrace. General Crittenden's father was the senior U.S. senator from Kentucky who in 1861 tried unsuccessfully to broker a compromise between the United States and the Confederacy.

Alexander McCook. *Perryville Battlefield State Historic Site.*

Crittenden's three divisions were all led by experienced brigadiers: John M. Palmer, Horatio Van Cleve and Thomas J. Wood.[42]

The Center Wing belonged to George Thomas. It was the largest part of the army, numbering five divisions under Major General Lovell H. Rousseau and Brigadier Generals James S. Negley, Speed Fry, Joseph J. Reynolds and Robert B. Mitchell. Rosecrans treated Thomas as a de facto second in command, and this large command was testament to Thomas's rank and experience. Not all of Center Wing's divisions left Nashville; Reynolds's and part of Fry's divisions guarded the roads and railroad north of the capital, while Mitchell's division stayed behind to garrison Nashville. These detachments meant that Rosecrans took only forty-six thousand men to meet Bragg.[43]

The Army of the Cumberland marched out of Nashville as a three-headed hydra, moving along parallel routes to snare the Confederates. Thomas's Center Wing followed the Franklin Road south out of Nashville, while McCook's command moved south along the Nolensville Pike toward Hardee's position at Triune. Crittenden's wing marched directly southeast along the Murfreesboro Road. Rosecrans expected Bragg to defend either the heights at Triune or along Murfreesboro Road at the ridges fronting Stewart's Creek, and his plan accounted for either possibility: "McCook was to attack Hardee

Thomas Crittenden. *Perryville Battlefield State Historic Site.*

at Triune, and, if the enemy re-enforced Hardee, Thomas was to support McCook. If McCook beat Hardee, or Hardee retreated, and the enemy met us at Stewart's Creek, 5 miles south of La Vergne, Crittenden was to attack him, Thomas was to come in on his left flank, and McCook…was to move with the remainder of his force on their rear."[44]

Ten miles out from Nashville, the Federals encountered Bragg's cavalry under Wheeler and Brigadier General John A. Wharton. The horsemen skirmished much of the day, stopping Crittenden's wing at La Vergne and delaying McCook in sharp fighting at Nolensville. Negley's division, leading Thomas's wing, heard the firing to the east at Nolensville and turned to assist. That afternoon it rained, turning damp roads into morasses. Except for New Year's Eve, the weather brought rain or sleet each day during the campaign.[45]

That evening, the Confederate high command learned of the Federal advance. Believing that he faced sixty thousand men, Bragg decided to concentrate for an engagement at Murfreesboro, ordering Hardee and McCown there on December 27. General Cleburne recalled that the Confederates "marched all day, part of it over a miserable road and through a cold, drenching rain," stopping for the night just outside Murfreesboro. The next day, Bragg sent a circular to all of his officers outlining his army's deployment; curiously, the last paragraph included instructions for use "should we be compelled to retire."[46]

Rain, fog and muddy roads conspired to delay the Army of the Cumberland's advance as much as Confederate cavalry. Aware that every mile he advanced lengthened his supply line to Nashville, Rosecrans looked for any indication of Bragg's intentions. Reports from McCook and Crittenden showed that the Confederates were falling back toward Murfreesboro and only opposing them with cavalry. Rosecrans now understood Bragg's true plans and decided to accept battle. After pausing on December 28 to consolidate, he set the army in motion for Murfreesboro.[47]

The Army of Tennessee covered the four main approaches to Murfreesboro from the west and north: the Franklin Road (also known

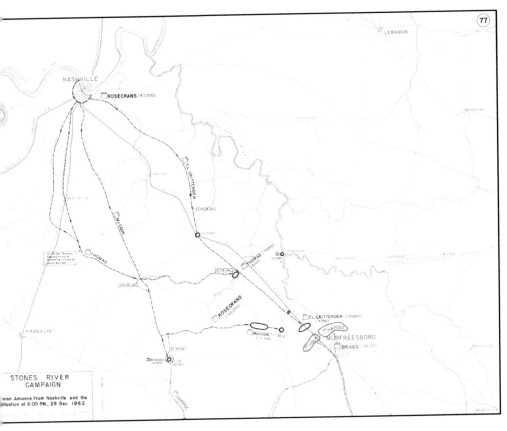

Rosecrans's advance from Nashville to Murfreesboro, December 26–30, 1862. From *West Point Atlas of American Wars. Author's collection.*

as Triune Road), the Wilkinson Turnpike, the Nashville Pike and parallel Nashville & Chattanooga Railroad and the Lebanon Road. Stones River flowed generally northwest–southeast, roughly paralleling the Nashville Pike. Because of the twists and turns of Stones River, Murfreesboro itself was on the opposite side of any potential battlefield; Bragg needed to straddle the river with his army to shield both the roads and his base in the town proper. The terrain around Murfreesboro was gently rolling and broken with stands of cedars. Polk's Corps and McCown's division took position on the south side of Stones River, while Hardee's men defended the opposite bank.[48]

On December 29 the first Federal elements, Crittenden's Left Wing, drew close to Murfreesboro. General Palmer observed movement in the Confederate line and mistakenly reported that Bragg was in retreat. Rosecrans

Charles Harker. *Perryville Battlefield State Historic Site.*

ordered Crittenden to take Murfreesboro, and Colonel Charles Harker's brigade crossed Stones River at McFadden's Ford to secure a promontory called Wayne's Hill and push into the city. Harker's Federals attacked the hill that afternoon, surprising a regiment of Breckinridge's division and driving it back. As dusk fell, the true situation became apparent, and Crittenden withdrew the brigade before it was destroyed by Hardee's two divisions. The next morning, McCook and Thomas arrived with their wings, and brisk skirmishing and artillery duels occurred along the front. Colonel John Beatty of Thomas's wing described December 30 as one of "our army...feeling its way into position." The Federal advance halted in late afternoon. "Tomorrow, doubtless, the grand battle will be fought," wrote Beatty, echoing the sentiments of many soldiers on both sides.[49]

As dusk settled on December 30, the armies faced each other in roughly parallel north–south lines about three miles west of Murfreesboro. Bragg's thirty-six thousand men stood in two lines, with Hardee's Corps (Breckinridge's and Cleburne's divisions) on the right around Wayne's Hill. Across the river, Polk arrayed his two divisions with Withers in the front line supported by Cheatham. McCown's division anchored the Confederate left. Wheeler's one thousand horsemen were detached and raiding along the pike connecting Rosecrans with Nashville. Rosecrans had left two infantry brigades totaling three thousand men to guard the wagon trains; his forty-three thousand Federals deployed opposite Bragg in a four-mile line from McFadden's Ford to the Franklin Pike. McCook held the right with the divisions of Johnson, Davis and Sheridan in line from south to north. Thomas posted in the center, with Negley's division in the front line and Rousseau in reserve. Crittenden straddled the Nashville Pike and the railroad with Palmer's, Wood's and Van Cleve's divisions.[50]

That night, both commanding generals examined the situation and came to the same conclusion: defend on the right and hit the enemy's left the next morning, December 31. In a conference, Rosecrans outlined his plan: send

Van Cleve and Wood across the river in a repeat of Harker's movement on the twenty-ninth. At the same time, Thomas's wing and Palmer's division would advance astride the Nashville Pike toward Murfreesboro. The crossing was to begin at about 7:00 a.m. the next morning, with the main attack scheduled for 8:00 a.m. McCook was enjoined to hold the right for at least three hours and do whatever necessary to make his line entirely secure. Rosecrans did not inspect his right flank, instead staying near the river. "I trusted General McCook's ability as to position, as much as I knew I could his courage and loyalty. It was a mistake," he admitted later.[51]

General Bragg also planned an attack of his own for the last day of 1862. He ordered Hardee to take Cleburne's division to the left and reinforce McCown for an advance at daylight. Wharton's cavalry would assist. "The attack [was then] to be taken up by Lieutenant General Polk's command in succession to the right flank, the move to be made to a constant wheel to the right, on Polk's right flank as a pivot, the object being to force the enemy back on Stone's River, and…cut him off from his base of operations and supplies by the Nashville pike," Bragg wrote. In essence, Bragg sought to fold Rosecrans's line in on itself like a closing jackknife.[52]

As dusk settled in, Cleburne's men set off on the cold and wet slog from one end of the army to the other. His men forded Stones River and marched to their assigned position, reaching it after midnight. Fires were forbidden for fear of tipping off the enemy, although the campfires of Polk's and Rosecrans's men were visible. After a few hours of rest, Cleburne woke his men at 4:30 a.m. to prepare. In front of his division stretched McCown's three brigades under Brigadier Generals James Rains, Matthew Ector and Evander McNair, overlapping the Union flank. Cleburne's four brigades under Brigadier Generals St. John R. Liddell, Bushrod R. Johnson, Lucius Polk and S.A.M. Wood took position in line and slightly to McCown's right rear. Bragg's plan called for McCown's men to lead the attack and Cleburne's troops to support it, keeping a tight mass of 10,500 men in the two divisions as they slashed the three and a half miles through Rosecrans's rear to the Nashville Pike. At 5:45 a.m., General Hardee made one final check with McCown and Cleburne to ensure that everything was in readiness. Shortly after 6:00 a.m., McCown's officers signaled the advance.[53]

Over in the Federal line, McCook's men were just awakening. McCook's right was held by Richard Johnson's division of three brigades. Brigadier General August Willich's outfit faced southwest along the Franklin Pike, while Brigadier General Edward N. Kirk's command faced south and southeast, with its right on the pike. To Kirk's rear ran Gresham Lane, a

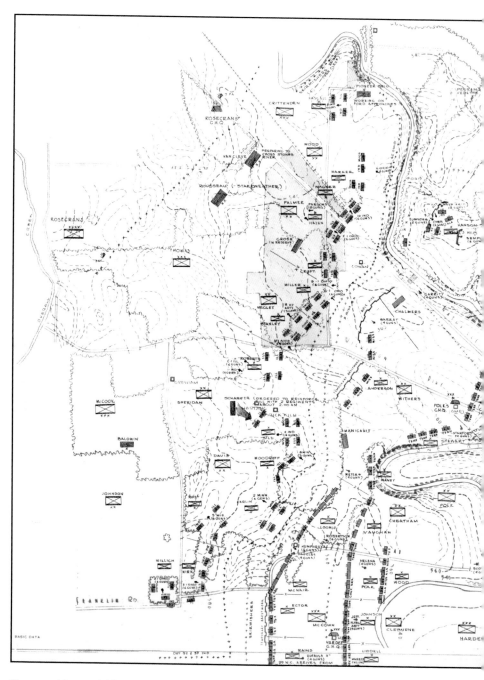

Troop positions at 6:00 a.m., December 31, 1862. *Stones River National Battlefield.*

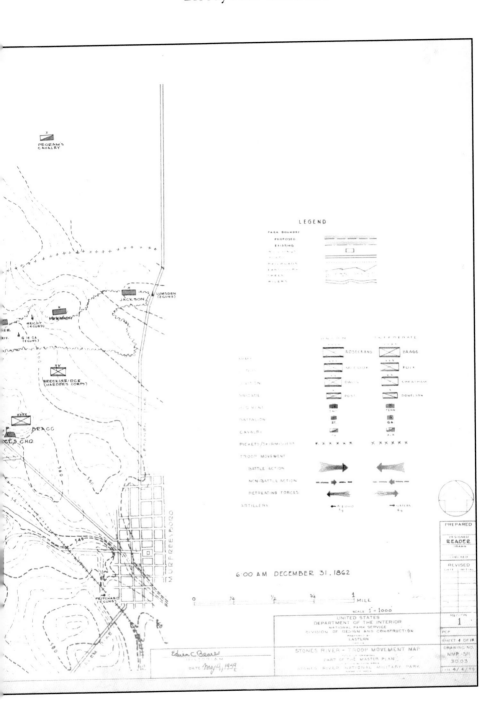

farm road that ran north to the Wilkinson Turnpike. In reserve a short distance back stood Colonel Philemon Baldwin's brigade. A sense of calm pervaded the camps as men leisurely made breakfast and drank coffee. Willich had patrolled the area before dawn with the 39th Indiana and found nothing. Artillery and wagon horses were being watered. The Confederates could not have planned a fuller surprise than what they got.[54]

At 6:25 a.m., the Confederate storm broke on Richard Johnson's troops. "The enemy advanced on our position with four heavy lines of battle, with a strong reserve

John McCown. *Library of Congress.*

held in mass," reported an Ohio officer in Willich's brigade. Desperate officers ordered their men into line, but the brigades only partially formed before McCown's men swarmed into the Federal camps. Some units tried to make a stand, but most men took to their heels. An Indianan described the scene: "Bull Run! You all know what it means. Now, McCook's corps had a second and improved edition…Confusion arose, a terrible panic gripped the troops." "Nothing could withstand the fury of the onset," commented Colonel R.W. Harper of the 1st Arkansas Rifles in McNair's brigade.[55]

Willich and Kirk both tried to rally their men to defend. General Willich's horse was shot and fell on top of him; in the confusion, the general was left to be captured. Leaderless and flanked, his brigade collapsed. Kirk put together a thin line that made a short stand, but it dissolved when the general suffered a mortal wound. The point-blank fighting caused some sharp losses in McCown's units, but the Southern momentum proved irresistible. "The enemy's lines were broken, and the rout, so far as my observation reached, became general," wrote Colonel Harper. By 7:00 a.m., McCook's right flank had collapsed. The Confederates captured so many prisoners that they simply ordered the masses rearward rather than slow their advance.[56]

As Willich's and Kirk's survivors fled northwestward, McCown's Confederates followed. "The force of the enemy to my front prevented me

Above: Willich's position in 2011, with the Franklin Road in the foreground. McCown's troops approached across the fields in the distance. *Photograph by Terry R. Woodson.*

Left: Edward Kirk. From *Battles and Leaders of the Civil War*, volume 3.

throwing forward my left wing as soon as instructed by Lieutenant General Hardee," admitted McCown. Instead of wheeling right, McCown's division sidled left and forced Cleburne's division into the front line. Instead of following each other across the battlefield as planned, Bragg's two spearhead divisions now fought abreast for the rest of the battle. The Confederate attack had been underway for less than an hour, and already the plan of a concentrated push had broken down.[57]

Cleburne's four brigades swung into action astride the Gresham Lane. This movement brought them into contact with Jefferson C. Davis's Federal division, deployed north of Kirk's position. Colonel Sidney Post's brigade held the division's left, Colonel William Carlin's brigade the center and Colonel William Woodruff's brigade the right. Post's brigade faced the greatest danger, as the retreat of Johnson's division exposed it to destruction. Pulling

Michael Gooding. *Perryville Battlefield State Historic Site.*

his troops back astride Gresham Lane, Post brought up the 5th Wisconsin Battery and Colonel Michael Gooding's 22nd Indiana to anchor the new line along a fence row.[58]

In the rear, Colonel Baldwin had heard the firing and formed his brigade west of Gresham Lane. From his position near a cedar stand, Baldwin observed the fugitives of the other brigades fleeing across his front. At this point, Richard Johnson appeared and sent the troops forward to defend a fence line. Taking position behind the fence, Baldwin's troops fronted what one Indiana officer described as a "stalk-field." He loosely linked his men with Post's troops to his left.[59]

Cleburne's division struck just as the Federals got into position. In response to a call for help from McCown, Liddell pushed his Arkansans toward the fence. His men advanced to within one hundred yards of Baldwin's infantry. The Federal fire, remembered Liddell, "was very trying. My men, seeing the great advantage to the enemy and the certain destruction awaiting them, dropped down, almost as if by common consent, on their faces, and commenced firing with great accuracy" on the enemy position.[60]

Meanwhile, Bushrod Johnson's Tennesseans clashed with Post's men astride Gresham Lane. "The enemy made their appearance in great numbers," remembered Colonel Gooding, "advancing in solid column."

Left: Patrick Cleburne. *Perryville Battlefield State Historic Site.*

Below: Looking south from Baldwin's position at the fence in 2011. The church steeple along the skyline marks Willich's position. The Confederates attacked across these fields. *Photograph by Terry R. Woodson.*

The 5th Wisconsin Battery opened what the 17th Tennessee's commander called a "galling fire." Nonetheless, the 17th pushed forward "in fine style to within 150 yards of the battery," according to one of its officers. "We halted and engaged them for some time to good effect." On the other side of Gresham Lane, Post's Federals and Bushrod Johnson's Confederates fought what Colonel John Fulton of the 44th Tennessee described as "a very severe engagement, fighting some twenty minutes before the enemy gave way."[61]

General Davis had other problems, for now the Confederates brought more units into action against his line. Wood's brigade attacked Carlin's troops, while Woodruff's men faced the first elements of Polk's Corps, in the form of Colonel J.Q. Loomis's brigade. Much of the Federal line stood in the cedars, which afforded some protection and also helped break up the Confederate formations. According to Davis, "These brigades were fully prepared for the attack, and received it with veteran courage. The conflict was fierce in the extreme on both sides. Our loss was heavy and that of the enemy no less."[62]

The battle raged for thirty minutes as both sides fought desperately. McNair's brigade of McCown's division shifted to support Liddell's troops, which finally caused McCown to wheel his units to the right and proceed with the original plan. McNair's troops formed for an assault at angles to Baldwin's line. Their appearance caused the Federals to waver, which

Bushrod Johnson. *Perryville Battlefield State Historic Site.*

William Carlin. *Perryville Battlefield State Historic Site.*

prompted a Confederate charge against the fence. Baldwin's line crumpled in confusion. "The right of the division was completely crushed in," recalled Lieutenant Colonel William Berry of the 5th Kentucky (U.S.). The Federals fled north.[63]

Baldwin's collapse unhinged Davis's entire position. Liddell's brigade swept over the fence, the general himself among the first across. Post's Federals fell back, covered by the 59th Illinois with fixed bayonets. Carlin's brigade gave way under pressure from his front and right, while Woodruff extricated his men and retired northward. Retreat soon turned into rout, with many men not stopping until reaching the Nashville Pike, three miles away. An estimated 25 percent of Davis's men had fallen in the thirty minutes of fighting.[64]

By 8:00 a.m., two hours into Bragg's offensive, Hardee's soldiers had routed two Federal divisions and now pressed toward the Nashville Pike. Despite some problems, the Confederate plan was unfolding well. But with most elements of both armies still unengaged, the battle was only beginning. New Year's Eve promised to be a bloody day.

Chapter 5

I Will Die Right Here

General Rosecrans started New Year's Eve at Left Wing headquarters near McFadden's Ford. He and his staff heard the firing on the right but thought little of it since they expected McCook to be fighting at that hour. Crittenden's advance began as planned at 7:00 a.m., as the lead elements of Van Cleve's division crossed at McFadden's Ford and deployed. Wood's division awaited its turn to cross. While Rosecrans watched the movement, at 7:30 a.m. a staff officer from McCook reported vaguely that "the right wing was heavily pressed and needed reinforcements." Not appreciating the true state of affairs, Rosecrans replied, "Tell him [McCook] to dispose his troops to best advantage and to hold his ground obstinately," and sent the officer back to Right Wing headquarters. "It is working right," Rosecrans announced to his staff.[65]

Thirty minutes later, another of McCook's staffers arrived with a more detailed report that gave a clearer picture of the Right Wing's disaster. This information, coupled with the appearance of stragglers and what Rosecrans called "the rapid movement of the noise of battle toward the north," caused the commanding general to momentarily go pale. Recovering his composure, he promised help to McCook and immediately recalled Van Cleve's men from across the river. Instead of attacking on the Federal left, the force around McFadden's Ford would be used to shore up the army's crumbling right. One brigade stayed behind to watch the crossing, while the rest of Van Cleve's division marched to the sound of the guns. Wood also detached some of his troops to help. These movements took time and were further stalled by mud and confusion along the Nashville Pike. At 9:00 a.m., Thomas received orders to send Rousseau's veteran division to help the Right Wing. Having thus dropped the original battle plan in order to save the army, General Rosecrans and his staff departed for the front to superintend the battle.[66]

Meanwhile, the fighting spread as more units of both armies swung into action. On the Confederate side, Withers's and Cheatham's divisions of Polk's Corps prepared to attack the portion of the Federal line stretching from Davis's former position to Stones River itself. Withers's troops deployed in front, with the brigades of Colonels John Q. Loomis and Arthur Manigault and Brigadier Generals J. Patton Anderson and James Chalmers arrayed from left to right. Behind them stood Cheatham's veterans, with Colonel A.J. Vaughan's troops behind Loomis on the left, followed by three brigades under Brigadier Generals George E. Maney, Alexander P. Stewart and Daniel S. Donelson extending the line to the river. To avoid command confusion, General Cheatham commanded the four left brigades while Withers directed the four on the right. The plan called for these troops to make an echelon attack from left to right, each lead unit attacking in stairstep fashion while the rear brigade supported the advance.[67]

Philip Sheridan's Federals stood opposite Loomis's and Manigault's troops. Alarmed by the Confederate activity opposite, Sheridan woke his men at

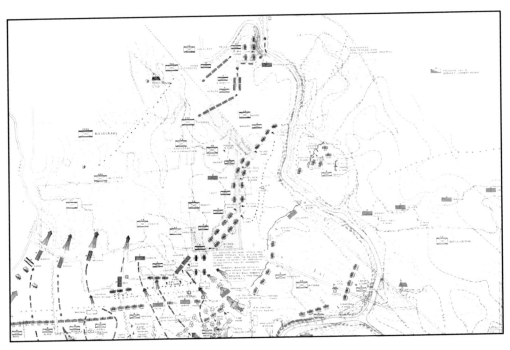

The Battle of Stones River, 9:00 a.m., December 31, 1862. *Stones River National Battlefield.*

Jones Withers. *Perryville Battlefield State Historic Site.*

Philip Sheridan. *Perryville Battlefield State Historic Site.*

4:30 a.m. to prepare for action at dawn. His line ran through some rolling and rocky terrain studded with woods. Unlike the other divisions of the Right Wing, this command was prepared for the Confederate attacks.

The first blows fell about 7:30 a.m. on Brigadier General Joshua Sill's brigade, holding Sheridan's right. "The enemy...attacked me, advancing

Joshua Sill. From *Battles and Leaders of the Civil War,* volume 3.

across an old cotton-field in Sill's front in heavy masses," recalled Sheridan. Federal artillery and infantry fire tore into the Confederates, wounding Loomis and causing the line to fall back. Vaughan's Confederates advanced in support, reaching the Union line and dislodging the 24th Wisconsin. The 44th Illinois and 15th Missouri counterattacked and restored the situation, prompting a general Federal countercharge that pushed into the Confederate lines. During the battle, General Sill fell at the head of his troops when a bullet smashed his face and entered his brain. He died without regaining consciousness. Colonel Nicholas Greusel of the 36th Illinois succeeded Sill in command of the brigade.[68]

Davis's division now collapsed, uncovering Sheridan's right. The Confederates proceeded to hit Sheridan's division from three directions. Cleburne's Confederates clawed at Greusel's right and rear, while Manigault's men pounded Sheridan's two other brigades under Colonels Frederick Schaefer and George Roberts. General Cheatham, who showed signs of inebriation, personally rallied Vaughan's troops and led them forward against Greusel's Federals. "This state of things would soon subject me to a fire in reverse," said Sheridan, and he looked for a solution. In a severe test of discipline, Sheridan's men executed a ninety-degree rearward turn under enemy assault. As Roberts's all-Illinois brigade counterattacked to cover the movement, Greusel and Schaefer pulled their men back to a new line facing south along a low ridge behind the Giles Harding House, anchored by the division's artillery along the left flank. "No hope of stemming the tide at this point seemed probable," remembered Sheridan, "but to gain time I retained my ground as long as possible." His stand was aided by elements of Davis's division that had rallied alongside and the fact that Cleburne's men now ran low on ammunition and paused to resupply.[69]

Right: Benjamin Cheatham.
Perryville Battlefield State Historic Site.

Below: Looking west along modern-day Medical Center Parkway in 2011. Sheridan's division defended the ridge in the right side of the picture against Cleburne's and Cheatham's attacks. *Photograph by Terry R. Woodson.*

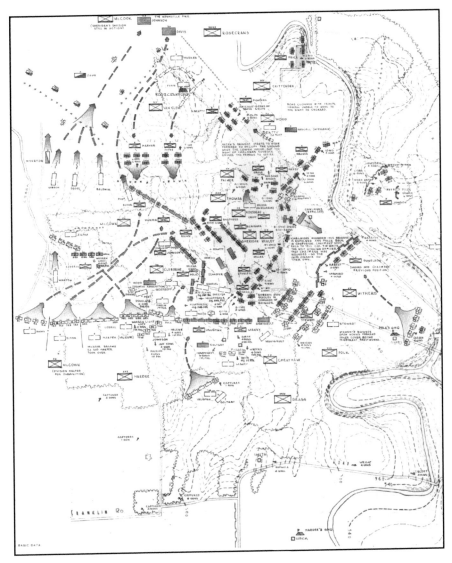

The Battle of Stones River, 10:00 a.m., December 31, 1862. *Stones River National Battlefield.*

Shortly before 10:00 a.m., Sheridan retired his division across the Wilkinson Pike, taking position in a large patch of cedars and rock outcroppings alongside Negley's veterans. The situation was critical; Lieutenant Arthur MacArthur of the 24th Wisconsin summed it up in a letter home: "At length we arrived in the woods, and here was a general retreat, and I would not have given a snap of my fingers for the whole army." Yet now the impact of Rosecrans's decision to strip his left began to be felt, as Federal reinforcements arrived to try and prevent the jackknife from closing.[70]

While the main infantry battle occurred between Sheridan and Cheatham, a mile west Cleburne's and McCown's Confederates pressed northward. Their rapid advance was punctuated by sharp skirmishes with disorganized enemy units, while several of Cleburne's brigades engaged the troops under Sheridan and Davis. Some of Liddell's men captured the Right Wing's main hospital, including the body of General Sill. The fire from Federal artillery and infantry had also pulled Cleburne's men westward. "I began to discover from the firing that I was getting in rear of the right flank of the enemy's center," said Cleburne. Concerned about getting too far behind the Federal line and becoming isolated, both divisions paused along the Wilkinson Pike to replenish ammunition. General McCown next angled his division northeastward toward the cedars beyond Sheridan's flank. Cleburne's division stayed in contact with the Federals and kept up the attack.[71]

A little north of the Wilkinson Pike, the cavalry of both sides grappled over possession of McCook's wagon train, a rich prize of ammunition, food and supplies. Captain Gates P. Thruston of McCook's staff had taken command of the seventy-six wagons and was leading them north along the Asbury Lane toward Asbury Church, where he hoped to turn right and head northeast to the Nashville Pike. Wharton's Confederate horsemen pursued the train, paralleling the course of Overall Creek to the west. Colonel Lewis Zahm's Federal cavalry brigade had just arrived to escort the wagons when Confederate shells opened on them from Wharton's horse artillery. "I determined to move across country, give the cavalry battle, and to attempt to capture the train," wrote Wharton. The 1st Confederate Cavalry galloped toward the enemy, brushing aside Zahm's 1st Ohio Cavalry and getting in among the wagons. Two of Zahm's other units (the 4th Ohio Cavalry and 2nd East Tennessee Cavalry) fled, but the 3rd Ohio Cavalry stood and fought a melee with the 1st Confederate, driving it back. Wharton committed more of his men into the fight against the Ohioans. At this point, Colonel John Kennett, the senior Federal cavalry officer on the field, rode in with the 3rd Kentucky and 4th U.S. Cavalry regiments, charged the Confederates and secured the wagons. Escorted by Federal horsemen, Thruston took the train to the Nashville Pike and safety.[72]

Meanwhile, Lovell Rousseau deployed his infantry division in the cedars to Sheridan's right. John Beatty's brigade led the march into what he described as "a cedar thicket so dense as to render it impossible to see the length of a regiment." As they took position, men of the 15th Kentucky (U.S.) and 42nd Indiana dislodged wild turkeys, a few of which were caught. "Hold it until hell freezes over," instructed Rousseau. Regular infantry of Lieutenant Colonel Oliver H. Shepherd's brigade formed to Beatty's right, supported by part of Colonel Benjamin Scribner's brigade. Rousseau's left tied loosely with Sheridan's troops, while his right dangled in the air.[73]

"Our lines were hardly formed before a dropping fire of the enemy announced his approach," reported Rousseau. Rains's brigade of McCown's division slammed into Shepherd's Regulars, while Lucius Polk's brigade of Cleburne's division hit Beatty's line. "Here the struggle of the day took place," recalled Colonel Robert B. Vance of the 29th North Carolina. "The enemy, sheltering themselves behind the trunks of the thickly standing trees and the large rocks, of which there were many, stubbornly contested the ground inch by inch."[74]

The powerful Confederate attacks strained the Union line, cracking it in places. Nineteen-year-old Colonel James B. Forman of the 15th Kentucky died in the fighting; his death caused the 15th to waver, exposing Rousseau's center. Ultimately, the Southerners fell back, repulsed by the weight of Union fire. As the enemy reformed, Rousseau became worried about his position and the possibility of being outflanked to the right, since the rest of McCown's infantry threatened to push past his flank. To Rousseau's rear across a cotton field stood the Nashville Pike—a knoll between the road and railroad dominated the area. This was the place to make a new stand. "I sent orders at once to my brigade commanders to fall back," recalled Rousseau. As that order went out for delivery, the Confederates struck again.[75]

While Rousseau's men fought in the cedars, the divisions of Sheridan and Negley struggled to hold open the jackknife's hinge. Because of the shape of the line, the Confederate attacks converged on the wooded rocky outcroppings along the Wilkinson Pike, defended by Sheridan's infantry and Negley's two brigades under Colonels Timothy R. Stanley and John F. Miller. Sheridan's artillery held the line's apex. The Federals sheltered in the woods and rocks while the Confederates approached across several hundred yards of open cotton field. As the action began, Rosecrans sent an order for Negley and Sheridan to hold at all costs, even if it meant their total destruction. "Every energy was therefore bent to simple holding of our ground," wrote Sheridan. For an hour, the Confederates hammered this area with concentrated artillery fire and repeated infantry charges from Manigault's, Maney's, Anderson's and Stewart's commands. Colonel Roberts died leading his men in the defense, the second of Sheridan's brigade commanders killed that day. The concentrated seesaw fighting earned the area the nickname the Slaughter Pen. The Union troops held on, repelling all attacks. The Confederates retired across the Wilkinson Pike and traded fire with the Federals in the woods. The fighting settled into a bloody stalemate.[76]

The cedars fighting upset Murfreesboro's wildlife; a 24th Wisconsin veteran noted that "it seemed as if all the birds and rabbits in that large field were looking for protection around our feet...so thick and fast did the rebels send their shot and shell after us that you might think it impossible for a bird to escape them." During the fighting, a Confederate saw a rabbit break for cover and head to the rear; calling after him, he said, "Go to it, cotton-tail; I'd run too if I hadn't a reputation."[77]

To Sheridan's right, Rousseau's men fought in the woods against growing Confederate pressure. Most of Rousseau's units had received the order to fall back and complied, but John Beatty's brigade had not and remained

The modern forest at Stones River National Battlefield still gives a sense of the thickness of the cedars in 1862. *Photograph by Terry R. Woodson.*

John Beatty. *Library of Congress.*

in position. His men fought on, repelling a charge and unaware of their growing isolation. The colonel learned of his predicament when a staff officer could not find Shepherd's Regulars or Scribner's troops. "I conclude that the contingency has arisen to which General Rousseau referred— that is to say, that hell had frozen over—and about face my brigade and march to the rear," recalled Beatty. The Confederates pursued, turning the retreat from the cedars into a rout. "The field [between the cedars and the Nashville Pike] is by this time covered with flying troops, and the enemy's fire is most deadly," remembered Beatty. The tide of retreat carried him and his troops back to the pike. There General Rousseau rallied the division and prepared a defense.[78]

Rousseau's retirement allowed the Confederates to sweep into the open field behind the divisions of Sheridan and Negley, threatening them with encirclement. To add to their problems, both commands were low on ammunition, Sheridan's division dangerously so. Negley ordered his division to "cut its way through," while Sheridan directed his men to fix bayonets and retire. Due to horse casualties, mud and crew fatigue, most of the artillery had to be left to the enemy. The rough terrain combined with Confederate pressure to disorder the Federal divisions. Leaders brought their units back in as good order as possible, but to an observer it looked like "ten thousand fugitives…burst from the cedar thickets and rushed into the open space between them and the turnpike." Many men

Negley's Federals sheltered behind these rocks, shown here in 2011. *Photograph by Terry R. Woodson.*

fell captured in the confusion, but the majority made it to the Nashville Pike. "We continued to press the enemy, fighting as we advanced, until we had driven them entirely out of the glade," recalled Colonel Otho Strahl of the 4th/5th Tennessee.[79]

As the cedars fight ended at about 11:00 a.m., the battle balanced on the knife edge as Rosecrans's Federals recoiled back to the Nashville Pike and Bragg's Confederates pursued. As each unit emerged from the cedars south of the Nashville Pike, most Confederates saw the road itself, the objective they were fighting to reach, for the first time. The Southern momentum slackened a bit as Cleburne's division angled left and started northward. But McCown's, Cheatham's and Withers's units continued to advance directly against the new Federal position. Victory was literally within sight.

Astute Confederates may have seen a group of officers on horseback dashing about the Federal line. It was General Rosecrans and his staff, riding around the battlefield giving advice, orders and encouragement to the troops, often under fire. Scores of Federals wrote of seeing the commanding general on his gray horse, an unlit cigar clamped between his teeth. Rosecrans's presence at the front heartened his army, as one officer later wrote: "I could not help expressing my gratitude to Providence for

The Regular Brigade
Monument, Stones River
National Cemetery, in 2011.
Photograph by Terry R. Woodson.

having given us a man who was equal to the occasion—a general in fact as well as in name." General Palmer later said, "If I was to fight a battle for the dominion of the universe, I would give Rosecrans the command of as many men as he could see and who could see him." Rosecrans also took time to visit McFadden's Ford, where Colonel Samuel Price's small brigade guarded the key crossing. "Will you hold this ford?" he queried Price. "I will try, sir," was the reply. "Will you hold this ford?" Rosecrans asked with more emphasis. "I will die right here," affirmed Price. "Will you hold this ford?" the general demanded again. "Yes, sir," came the answer. "That will do," replied Rosecrans, who rode off.[80]

General Rosecrans now met Sheridan's men falling back and ordered them to replenish their ammunition and support Palmer's and Wood's troops astride the pike. Eighteen Federal artillery pieces now studded the small knoll between the Nashville Pike and the railroad, anchoring the Federal defense. Riding over to help rally Rousseau's men, Rosecrans put the Pioneer Brigade on the knoll and personally directed Van Cleve's

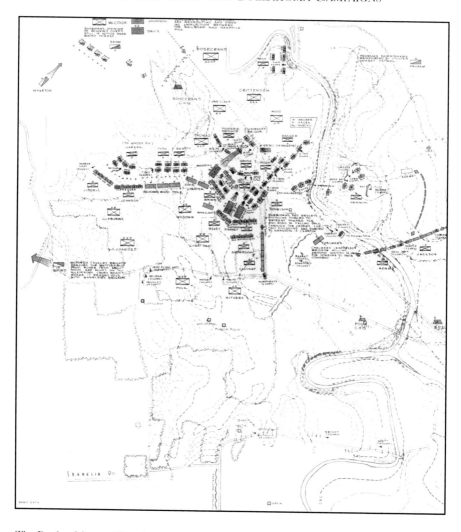

The Battle of Stones River between 11:00 a.m. and 1:00 p.m., December 31, 1862. *Stones River National Battlefield.*

men into position on the far right. The first Confederates, in the form of Rains's brigade, now hit the Union line. Erupting from the cedars in pursuit of Rousseau's veterans, Rains bravely led his command forward on horseback. "Here was the struggle for the day, and a hard one it was," recalled Colonel Vance. Rains fell dead from his horse, which caused some confusion in his units. "They came on like demons," recalled a Regular. The artillery fire made "gap after gap in their ranks. The fire was rather too hot to suit them and what few of them was left came to an about face

James Rains. From *Battles and Leaders of the Civil War*, volume 3.

and skedaddled back to the cedar woods for shelter."[81]

During this action, Palmer's Federals shattered a Confederate charge up the Nashville Pike by Chalmers's Mississippi brigade. Further Confederate attacks battered Palmer's division, forcing his right brigade back parallel to the pike. Lieutenant Charles Parsons's battery anchored the turn, firing in two directions. On the knoll, Rosecrans realized that he needed to buy time to coalesce his new line along the pike. Turning to General Thomas, he made the coldblooded decision to send the Regular Brigade back into the cedars to trade their lives for the necessary time. Thomas gave a terse order to Lieutenant Colonel Shepherd: "Shepherd, take your brigade in there and stop the Rebels." The 1,400 professionals of the 15th, 16th, 18th and 19th United States Infantry Regiments marched across the cotton field into Negley's former position.[82]

Meanwhile, A.P. Stewart organized what units he could find and plunged them into the cedars. Shepherd's Regulars collided with Stewart's force. Badly outnumbered, the Regulars stood their ground, firing by file and raking the Confederate lines. "The first line of the enemy were scattered like chaff," recalled a Regular. Yet the enemy also struck back. "Our men were close upon them, and every shot did its work," recalled Colonel Strahl. For twenty minutes, the unequal firefight raged, until Shepherd "thought it proper to order a retreat, which was probably long enough deferred." Two regiments personally led by General Rousseau helped cover the rapid Federal retirement across the fire-swept cotton field to the Nashville Pike. When Shepherd rallied his men and counted them, only 806 answered the rolls. In forty-five minutes, the Regular Brigade had lost 44 percent of its members.[83]

But the Regulars' sacrifice was not in vain; they had bought enough time for Rosecrans to set his army in position along the Nashville Pike. The Army of the Cumberland now stood in line running half a mile from Stones River to the pike and along it for a mile and a half. Artillery along the rise between the railroad and the pike commanded virtually the entire position. Infantrymen stood atop the knoll and the railroad embankment or took shelter in the depressed roadbed as a natural earthwork. Behind the pike and railroad flowed Stones River. The jackknife was almost closed. There could be no more retreat for the Federals.

Now, as the last afternoon of 1862 began, Bragg's Confederates sought to break this final position and win the day.

Chapter 6

This Army Does Not Retreat

As the clock passed noon on December 31, 1862, the Confederate situation looked promising. Bragg's men had pushed the Federals back over three miles and stood within a few hundred yards of cutting the Nashville Pike. McCown's and Cleburne's divisions continued to press ahead toward the pike, while Polk's forces had dislodged almost all of the Federal troops from their original positions. Yet all was not well in the Army of Tennessee's ranks, and several factors now combined to blunt the Confederate edge.

Bragg's grand offensive was breaking down. Hardee's spearhead units had been marching and fighting with scarcely a break for nearly six hours; among the reports of his corps, the words "jaded" and "tired" can be found to describe the troops' condition as they approached the Nashville Pike. They had outstripped their supplies and left their artillery behind. The terrain had broken up formations, causing units to intermix and slalom across the battlefield. Leader losses further disordered units of both Polk's and Hardee's commands. Bragg could be proud of his army's accomplishments, but his men were running out of steam. Hardee later lamented, "If, at the moment when the enemy were driven from the thick woods north of the Wilkinson turnpike [the cedars], a fresh division could have replaced Cleburne's troops and followed up the victory, the rout of Rosecrans' army would have been complete."[84]

Fresh troops were available, in the form of Breckinridge's six thousand men on the other side of Stones River. In contrast to his active counterpart Rosecrans, Bragg passively remained in the rear and left tactical direction of the battle to Polk and Hardee. Once the battle started, Bragg's key task was to monitor the situation and decide the best use of Breckinridge's division. He could hold it in place, send it across the river to Polk or Hardee or attack McFadden's Ford. Breckinridge himself had a responsibility to watch his front and give Bragg the necessary information to make the best choice. The mismanagement of this division ultimately cost Bragg the battle.

That morning, Breckinridge had his skirmishers and Brigadier General John Pegram's attached cavalry scouting to his front. The horsemen detected Van Cleve's initial movement across Stones River. However, Pegram's Confederates missed the Union withdrawal; at 10:10 a.m., Breckinridge reported that "the enemy are undoubtedly advancing upon me." Bragg ordered an advance toward McFadden's Ford but quickly countermanded the order, instead asking that two brigades be sent to Hardee to keep up his momentum. Fearing an attack, Breckinridge did not detach any troops. At 12:50 p.m., Breckinridge was still seeing chimerical Federal troops on his side of the river but finally sent the requested brigades. Judging the hour too late to get the reinforcements to Hardee, Bragg attached them to Polk. Still later, Bragg ordered Breckinridge and two more brigades to cross and join the main battle in Polk's sector.[85]

The what-ifs for this division abound. If the Confederate cavalry had scouted better, they would have detected the Federal withdrawal, and the infantry could have moved earlier to Hardee or Polk. A tantalizing and bold option would have been to press the attack against Price's troops at McFadden's Ford; a push across at that place would have put Rosecrans in a serious bind and would possibly have collapsed the entire Federal army. Even without beating Price's troops, such an action would have forced Rosecrans to divert men to his left during the critical midmorning hours in the cedars and along the pike, possibly weakening the main Federal line to a point beyond retrieval. But boldness was not in Bragg or Breckinridge that day, and instead Breckinridge's men went into action late and against the wrong place.

Meanwhile, Bragg's men came up against the final Federal line. In the center, Stewart's command reached the edge of the cedars. Federal artillery opened on the Confederate infantry. "For some time we were exposed to a terrific fire of shell, canister, and spherical case," recalled Stewart. "Having no battery of our own, and being nearly out of ammunition, it was impossible to proceed farther." Stewart's requests for artillery support were unavailing, and he had to be content with skirmishing in the field. "It is believed that if a battery could have been put in position…the enemy could have been shelled from their shelter in the ravine [roadbed] and behind the railroad, and the day might thus have been more completely ours," lamented an officer of the 19th Tennessee.[86]

Off to Stewart's left, McCown's tired division summoned one last effort to reach the pike. Rains's shattered brigade rallied to the rear, but Ector's and McNair's commands pressed ahead. Rosecrans personally led the Pioneer

Brigade against them, supported by elements of Rousseau's division. "No time was now to be lost, as the enemy had evidently made this their last stand-point, and opened on us with artillery and musketry," reported Colonel Harper. General McCown launched the two brigades into a headlong charge toward the Federal line.[87]

"The enemy's lines, with banners flying, came in sight on the verge of the timber, within 500 yards of our battery," recalled Lieutenant Alanson J. Stevens of Battery B, Pennsylvania Light Artillery. "We opened on them with spherical case, shell, and canister." Noted an Ohio infantryman: "As they move forward it looks as if there was no withstanding their advance." General Ector remembered the effect of the Union shelling: "The cedars were falling and being trimmed by bombs, canister, and iron hail, which seemed to fill the air." The Confederate infantry pushed to within fifty yards of the pike, but the Federal fire proved too much. "After ten or twelve minutes of the severest fighting it has ever been my lot to witness we were compelled to fall back with very heavy loss," said Colonel Harper. McCown's men rallied and took up a defensive position in the woods. Rosecrans's center was safe.[88]

The next crisis developed on the Federal right, as Patrick Cleburne's division slashed northward toward the Nashville Pike. Half a mile from their objective, Cleburne's men ran into Van Cleve's division, plus Harker's brigade of Wood's division. "No sooner had I taken position…than a most vigorous engagement commenced," recalled Harker. Liddell's Arkansans and Bushrod Johnson's Tennesseans faced Harker, while Vaughn's brigade and the rest of Cleburne's division engaged Van Cleve's troops. Both battle lines blazed away less than one hundred yards apart. After twenty minutes

Rosecrans's Federals stand along the Nashville Pike against McCown's and Withers's Confederates. From *Battles and Leaders of the Civil War*, volume 3.

of close-quarter combat, the Federals retired. "The enemy fled, leaving a long line of dead and wounded on the ground," recalled General Liddell. "We moved forward together toward the cedars on the turnpike and railroad with the enemy in full retreat before us. The general [Bushrod Johnson] and I congratulated each other on our success up to this time."[89]

On the cusp of victory, everything unraveled for the Confederates. As Cleburne's skirmishers reached the Nashville Pike, Van Cleve and Harker rallied their commands and charged the division's center and right, led by the 13th Michigan, 13th Ohio and the 59th Ohio. Surprised by this sudden surge, Cleburne's exhausted infantry faltered and fell back. Other units retired also, even though not engaged. "Men were falling back to the rear from right towards the left, and my senior colonel, Govan, thought it was a general understanding to do so," remembered Liddell. A frustrated Johnson recalled, "It was reported that our right was flanked by a heavy force. A precipitate retreat immediately followed…The movement was to me totally unexpected, and I have yet to learn that there existed a cause commensurate with the demoralization that ensued. At the moment in which I felt the utmost confidence in the success of our arms I was almost run over by our

Van Cleve's division stands against Cleburne's Confederates. From *Battles and Leaders of the Civil War*, volume 3.

retreating troops." After rallying a short distance to the rear, Hardee ordered a halt at 3:00 p.m. "It would have been folly, not valor, to assail them in this position," he explained. After more than eight hours of marching and fighting, Cleburne's division came to a halt mere yards short of its objective.[90]

These efforts spent, the battle's focus now shifted to the Federal left, the only part of the line still in its original location. Anchoring the position was a four-acre circular cedar brake known to both sides as the Round Forest. The wood itself stood on a slight elevation, forcing the Confederates to approach it along a flat stretch of ground running seven hundred yards eastward. A small house owned by the Cowan family near the forest offered the only protection. If the Round Forest fell, the entire Federal position would be flanked and tumble like dominoes. This sector was held by Palmer's division of three brigades under General Cruft, Colonel William B. Hazen and Colonel William Grose; Wood's division with Brigadier General Milo Hascall's and Colonel George D. Wagner's brigades; and other scratch elements of Rosecrans's army. Artillery bolstered the Federal line. Sheridan's division, restocked with ammunition, also received orders to assist the defense.[91]

Palmer's Federals had been scheduled to attack at 8:00 a.m. but were called back at the last minute. That morning, Chalmers's Mississippi brigade had

tested the position and shattered against the Federal defense. At noon, Donelson's Tennesseans had launched an attack. The Cowan House broke up the brigade formation, with the 16th Tennessee angling right while the other troops went to the left. Combined with Stewart's troops to his left, Donelson's men managed to dislodge most of Palmer's division, forcing the brigades of Grose and Cruft back to the Nashville Pike. Meanwhile, the 16th Tennessee's 377 men kept up what Colonel John Savage called "the fight against superior numbers with great spirit and obstinacy." The Federals outnumbered the Tennesseans ten to one. Supported by eighteen cannons, they mowed

Charles Cruft. *Perryville Battlefield State Historic Site.*

William Hazen. *Perryville Battlefield State Historic Site.*

George Wagner. *Perryville Battlefield State Historic Site.*

down the 16th, pinning the Confederates and eventually forcing them to withdraw. "Thirty men were left dead upon the spot where they halted, dressed in perfect line of battle. It was…a sad spectacle, speaking more eloquently for the discipline and courage of the men than any words I could employ," remembered Savage. After more than an hour, most of Donelson's Tennesseans withdrew from the

John Savage. *Perryville Battlefield State Historic Site.*

fight, although the 16th held on for two more hours, losing 207 men.[92]

Now only the brigades of Hazen, Wagner and Hascall occupied the original Federal position. Hazen's men held the Round Forest itself, with Wagner's troops posted to the left supported by Hascall's brigade. During a short lull, Rosecrans shifted Sheridan's men to assist Hazen, while Wood put Hascall's troops into the front line on either side of the Round Forest. Confederate artillery from Wayne's Hill played over the lines, keeping the defenders alert. The first two of Breckinridge's brigades, under Brigadier Generals Daniel W. Adams and John K. Jackson, reported to Polk at about 1:30 p.m.. The bishop decided to use them, as he later explained, "to drive in the enemy's left and especially, to dislodge him from his position in the Round Forest. Unfortunately, the opportune moment for putting in these detachments had passed." Nonetheless, Polk decided to proceed with the plan. General Bragg was observing from the rear and could have countermanded these attack orders, but he took no action.[93]

Polk next compounded his error by committing the units piecemeal against the Round Forest. Instead of attacking with both brigades simultaneously, or waiting for the rest of Breckinridge's force, which was due to arrive in an hour, Polk threw his men forward as quickly as they deployed. First in was Adams's Louisiana and Alabama command. As the brigade advanced with flags flying, the Cowan House forced a shift to the right, which pushed the attack directly against Hazen's and Wagner's troops. The defenders greeted Adams's Confederates with a "terrible fire," according to General Adams. His men halted and started a firefight with the Federals, which lasted until a flanking column threatened to cut

Right: Daniel Adams. *Perryville Battlefield State Historic Site.*

Below: The Battle of Stones River, about 2:30 p.m., December 31, 1862. *Stones River National Battlefield.*

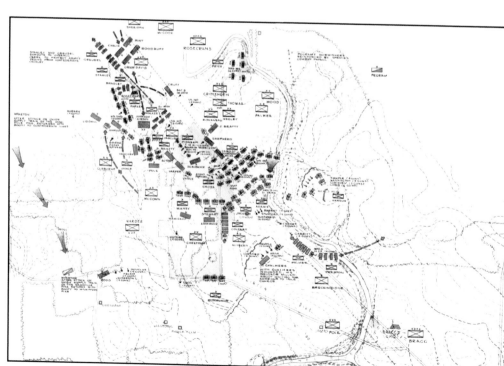

off the brigade. "Finding that I was overpowered in numbers…I had reluctantly to give the order to fall back," said Adams. The Confederates fled the field in disorder, having tried to do what General Adams called "more than any brigade could accomplish, and full work for a division, well directed." Adams himself fell wounded, and command passed to Colonel Randall L. Gibson.[94]

As Adams's Confederates fought on, Jackson's troops advanced to the left of the Cowan House. "A most destructive fire was opened upon them," recalled a Kentuckian in Hazen's brigade. The 73rd Illinois and 2nd Missouri of Sheridan's division came to help, losing Colonel Schaefer killed in the process, the third of Sheridan's three brigade commanders to die that day. Meanwhile, Jackson struggled to keep up the Confederate attack: "Twice I ordered a charge upon the enemy's strong position, but for the want of support from others, and the smallness of my own

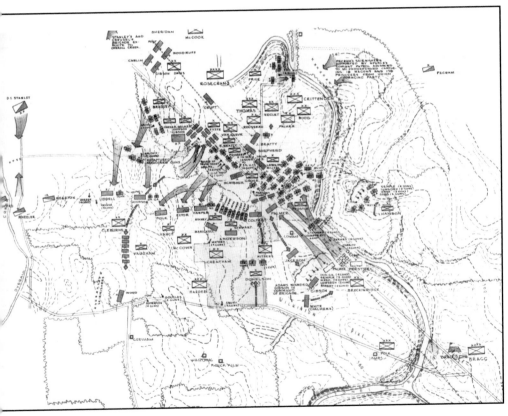

The Battle of Stones River at 4:00 p.m., December 31, 1862. *Stones River National Battlefield.*

numbers, was forced to take the cover of a thick cedar wood." By 3:00 p.m., both Confederate brigades had retired, leaving one-third of their men as casualties on the field.[95]

"A period of about one hour now ensued with but little infantry firing, but a murderous shower of shot and shell was rained from several directions upon this position," recalled Hazen. Bursts in the trees made splinters as deadly as shrapnel; most of Hazen's men lay prone to avoid the worst effects of the fire. Rosecrans toured the line with General Hascall, encouraging the men and directing the placement of reinforcements. Over in the Confederate lines, Breckinridge reported to Polk with the brigades of Brigadier General William Preston and Murfreesboro resident and former mayor Colonel Joseph B. Palmer. The bishop ordered them to form for a mass attack against the Round Forest. As soon as the troops took position, Polk sent them forward.[96]

Hazen later recalled the spectacle of Breckinridge's advance: "At about 4 p.m. the enemy again advanced upon my front in two lines. The battle had hushed, and the dreadful splendor of this advance can only be conceived, as all description must fall vastly short." Federal artillery and infantry tore

The Hazen Monument stands by the Round Forest and is the oldest Civil War monument still in its original location. It was raised by the brigade's veterans in 1863. This view was taken in 2011. *Photograph by Terry R. Woodson.*

into the massed Confederates, making a noise so intense that men from both sides picked cotton from the field to plug their ears against the din. "The several regiments of my brigade moved gallantly and steadily forward in this charge, although exposed to a terrible fire," wrote Colonel Palmer.[97]

Rosecrans, Thomas, McCook, Crittenden and their staffs watched this action from the knoll, in full view of troops on both sides. Confederate shellfire sought the suspicious group of mounted men, and Thomas and McCook soon broke away for safety. Oblivious to the shelling, General Rosecrans sensed that Hazen needed help. He spurred his horse toward the Round Forest, his staff following. Suddenly, a shell whistled past Rosecrans's head and decapitated his close friend and chief of staff, Lieutenant Colonel Julius P. Garesche. Garesche's headless body continued on horseback for another twenty paces and then slumped to the ground, his blood spattering on Rosecrans. Sheridan recalled that this horrible public death "stunned us all, and a momentary expression of horror spread over Rosecrans' face; but at such time the importance of self-control was vital, and he pursued his course with an appearance of indifference."[98]

The Confederate attack faltered as General Rosecrans reached the Round Forest. Breckinridge's men fell back in confusion before the concentrated Federal fire, and the final dusk of 1862 ended the fighting. "The day closed, leaving us masters of the original ground on our left," wrote Rosecrans.[99]

That night, both commanders took stock. It had been a very bloody day; the Army of the Cumberland had sustained more than 25 percent casualties and lost twenty-eight cannons while being pushed repeatedly to the edge of destruction. Five brigade leaders were casualties, along with two division commanders (Wood and Van Cleve, both wounded in the afternoon). On the other hand, plenty of ammunition remained for another day's engagement, and the two brigades that had been guarding supplies had fought their way through Wheeler's horsemen to join the army. Rosecrans called a meeting of his commanders, which occurred in a free-form manner that later produced conflicting accounts. Several generals preferred retirement, while others were noncommittal. Rosecrans himself appeared unsure of what to do. At one point, he scouted the army's right with McCook and returned satisfied of its strength. General Thomas turned the discussion by declaring, "This army does not retreat." Rosecrans agreed, telling his men, "Go to your commands and prepare to fight and die here." He consolidated and reorganized the Army of the Cumberland's lines, abandoned the Round Forest and had his men dig in. A wagon train of wounded departed for Nashville under strong escort.[100]

For his part, Bragg was ecstatic at the day's results. Despite losing more than eight thousand men, the Army of Tennessee had driven a larger Federal army several miles and came excruciatingly close to total success. That night, Bragg wrote to Richmond:

> *We assailed the enemy at 7 o'clock this morning [sic], and after ten hours' hard fighting have driven him from every position except his extreme left, [where] he has successfully resisted us. With the exception of this point, we occupy the whole field. We captured 4,000 prisoners, including 2 brigadier generals, 31 pieces of artillery, and some 200 wagons and teams. Our loss is heavy; that of the enemy's much greater.*

This dispatch, with its implicit promise of decisive victory, heartened the Confederacy as the new year dawned. Bragg appeared convinced that Rosecrans would retreat; movement of Federal troops and wagons seemed to reinforce the idea. He called no council of war and issued no orders for the next day.[101]

Not every Confederate general shared Bragg's complacency. Over on the Confederate left, General Liddell scouted the Federal line and detected a weak point. Seeing Hardee later, Liddell asked for reinforcements and proposed an attack toward Murfreesboro. "From some cause, Hardee would not listen to me, saying 'he was disgusted.' I gave it up and visited my wounded son in Murfreesboro during the night," remembered Liddell. "I have ever afterwards blamed myself for not going to see Bragg in person and persuading him to come and look for himself. It would have resulted in my failure, though, with no thanks…Bragg did not know whom to trust. He was not popular with his generals, hence, I feared that zealous cooperation on their part was wanting."[102]

New Year's Day 1863 dawned cold and rainy. Both sides skirmished as the Confederates determined the Federal position and intentions. Wheeler's cavalry continued its fourth straight day of attacking Federal wagon trains on the road between Nashville and Murfreesboro, disrupting Rosecrans's supply line. Many Federals searched for food, not having eaten since the night of December 30. In the afternoon, Van Cleve's division (now led by Colonel Samuel Beatty) crossed Stones River and occupied a wooded ridge overlooking McFadden's Ford and half a mile from Wayne's Hill. For his part, General Bragg later summed up January 1: "The whole day…was passed without an important movement on either side, and was consumed by us in gleaning the battlefield, burying the dead, and replenishing ammunition."[103]

January 2 opened with similar weather. The Army of Tennessee remained passive, drawing back from the Federals in places to consolidate. Confederate artillery probed Rosecrans's lines during the morning. Bragg realized that Samuel Beatty's division on the ridge held a key advantage. "Lieutenant General Polk's line was both commanded and enfiladed. The dislodgement of this force or the withdrawal of Polk's line was an evident necessity." Bragg decided to recapture the ridge.[104]

Breckinridge's division had recrossed piecemeal since the night of December 31 and received orders to attack toward McFadden's Ford. Wharton's and Pegram's cavalry would support Breckinridge's infantry, as would an artillery battalion under Captain Felix H. Robertson. General Breckinridge protested that the mission was impossible to execute, but Bragg refused to listen. Breckinridge's fatalistic view of the attack's prospects infected preparations; the general spent most of his time deploying the four infantry brigades that would participate (the Orphan

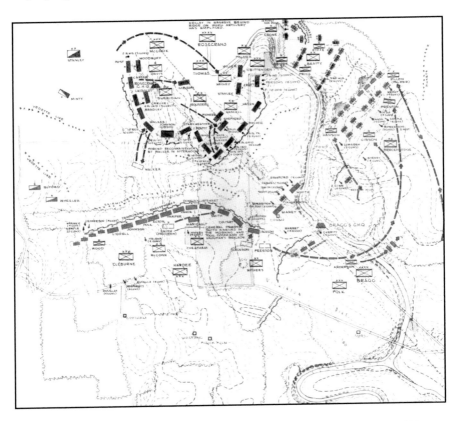

The Battle of Stones River at 4:00 p.m., January 2, 1863. *Stones River National Battlefield.*

Stones River at McFadden's Ford, seen at 4:30 p.m. on a January afternoon in 2011. *Photograph by Terry R. Woodson.*

Brigade under Brigadier General Roger W. Hanson, Preston's brigade and Brigadier General Gideon J. Pillow's brigade from left to right, with Gibson's troops in support). He made little effort to communicate or coordinate with the cavalry deployed on the infantry's right. Breckinridge also got into a hot dispute with Robertson over employment of the artillery; Robertson wanted to advance his guns after the objective was secure, while Breckinridge wanted the batteries to move forward alongside his infantry. Bragg's chief of staff was nearby but refused to referee, and the dispute was not resolved.[105]

At 4:00 p.m., Breckinridge signaled the advance. "Instantly the troops moved forward at a quick step…The front line had bayonets fixed, with orders to deliver one volley, and then use the bayonet," he reported. Beatty's two frontline brigades, under Colonels Price and James P. Fyffe, absorbed the first shock. The Confederates drove Price's men "backwards like fall leaves before a wintry wind; one after another the lines were swept away," wrote Fyffe. Beatty committed his reserve brigade, which held up Hanson's advance for a short time in a battle that pitted Kentuckian against Kentuckian. Some of Gibson's Louisianans came forward and broke the line, forcing the Federals back toward McFadden's Ford in disorder. Most

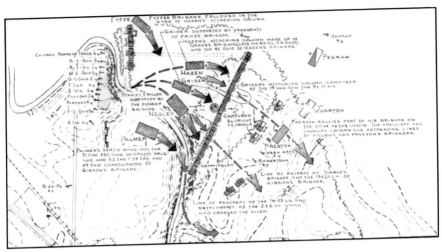

The Federal counterattack against Breckinridge's charge, January 2, 1863. *Stones River National Battlefield.*

of Beatty's division retired across Stones River, but Fyffe's troops and Colonel Grose's brigade formed a small perimeter just downstream of McFadden's Ford. In twenty minutes of fighting, Breckinridge's division had achieved its objective.[106]

The Confederates now pushed their luck too far, as Breckinridge's infantry chased the Federals down the ridge's rear slope into the open area opposite McFadden's Ford. General Crittenden watched the advance from the other side of Stones River. He turned to Captain John Mendenhall, the Left Wing's chief of artillery. "Now, Mendenhall, you must save my men with your cannon," he said. In short order, Mendenhall lined fifty-seven guns on a bluff overlooking the ford. They opened a concentrated bombardment on the Confederates that shook the ground. "[The enemy's] batteries concentrated on every spot from which he was driven," recalled Colonel Gibson. The constricted geography and Federal fire caused confusion in Confederate ranks, although several small groups of Kentuckians and Floridians crossed the river.[107]

While Mendenhall's artillery held the line, Federal infantry reinforcements arrived in the form of Negley's division, the Pioneer Brigade and two brigades under Hazen and Cruft. Samuel Beatty also rallied his men to aid in the defense. After a short firefight, Negley's men charged, followed by Hazen's and Beatty's troops. "From a rapid advance, [the enemy] broke at once into a rapid retreat," wrote Crittenden. A

Left: This monument marks the position of Mendenhall's guns on January 2. *Photograph by Terry R. Woodson.*

soldier in the 41st Ohio of Hazen's brigade wrote, "When the Forty-first had got over [the river], the ground in front was covered with crowds of men from both sides...Breckinridge's scattered men, of course, made little show of resistance, but took themselves off." Hazen's men pursued, firing a few volleys into the gathering dusk. The Federals regained all of the lost ground, capturing three Confederate cannons in the process. Gibson's troops covered the Confederate withdrawal as nightfall ended the fighting. "My poor Orphans!" cried Breckinridge as he watched his men spill back. In less than one hour, Breckinridge's division had sustained 1,400 casualties. "The news of this disastrous charge, led by the elite of the Confederate army, cast a gloom over all," remembered one of Bragg's staff officers.[108]

Breckinridge's abortive attack ended the Battle of Stones River, the Civil War's bloodiest battle by percentage of loss. More than one out of every four men on both sides who fought in the battle was killed, wounded or captured. In three days of fighting, Rosecrans lost 13,249 men killed, wounded, missing or captured of 46,000 men on the field, a 28 percent loss rate. Bragg's army engaged 37,000 and sustained 27 percent casualties, or 10,266 men.[109]

As night fell on January 2, the mangled armies eyed each other in the mud and rain. The battlefield appeared to be stalemated. But now the Army of Tennessee's high command began to crack wide open.

Chapter 7
Corrosion of an Army

That evening, General Bragg ordered reinforcements to help Breckinridge and went to sleep. An aide woke him at 2:00 a.m. on January 3 with a message from Generals Cheatham and Withers:

> We deem it our duty to say to you frankly that, in our judgment, this army should be promptly put in retreat. You have but three brigades [the intended word was "divisions"] that are at all reliable, and even some of these are more or less demoralized from having some brigade commanders who do not possess the confidence of their commands. Such is our opinion, and we deem it a solemn duty to express it to you. We do fear great disaster from the condition of things now existing, and think it should be averted if possible.

General Polk had endorsed the note, stating, "I am compelled to add that after seeing the effect of the operations of today, added to that produced upon the troops by the battle of the 31ˢᵗ, I very greatly fear the consequences of another engagement at this place on the ensuing day." Bragg read the first part of the message and told the messenger, "Say to the general we will hold our position at every hazard." Polk informed Hardee of the message and reply.[110]

Daylight brought a new cast to the situation as Bragg met with Polk and Hardee at 10:00 a.m. The news was not good for the Army of Tennessee. McCook's headquarters papers had been captured, and they showed a Federal strength of seventy thousand men. Wheeler's cavalry also reported the arrival of reinforcements with a large supply train from Nashville, which portended a possible Union offensive. Meanwhile, a heavy rain fell with no letup, threatening to raise the water level in Stones River and isolate the Army of Tennessee's two corps from each other. Polk and Hardee advised retreat, and Bragg concurred. At noon, the wagons and supplies were ordered southward.[111]

That night, Bragg's infantry stole away under cover of Wheeler's cavalry, which withdrew in the early morning hours of January 5. Rosecrans occupied Murfreesboro that day. Fearing a pursuit, Bragg originally planned to stop at Decherd on the Elk River but instead halted his army along the Highland Rim, fifteen miles southeast of Murfreesboro. Army headquarters was set up in Tullahoma, while Polk's Corps camped at Shelbyville and Hardee's troops posted around Wartrace.[112]

On January 5, Rosecrans telegraphed to the War Department in Washington: "God has crowned our arms with victory. Our enemy are

This monument marks the approximate location of Bragg's headquarters in Tullahoma. Bragg commanded the Army of Tennessee with the rank of general. *Photograph by Terry R. Woodson.*

badly beaten, and in full retreat. We shall press them as rapidly as our means of traveling and subsistence permit." To Halleck he wrote that Stones River was "one of the greatest battles of the war." Congratulations flowed in from all over the United States, including from President Lincoln, who telegraphed: "God bless you, and all with you! Please tender to all, and accept for yourself, the nation's gratitude for your and their skill, endurance, and dauntless courage."[113]

Rosecrans considered further pursuit but elected to halt in Murfreesboro. He needed to rectify his supply lines, which were in disarray. The railroad to Nashville required repairs, and the muddy Nashville Pike was inadequate to supply his army for active operations. John Hunt Morgan had cut the L&N in several places during his famed Christmas Raid, severing Rosecrans's main logistical lifeline yet again. The Army of the Cumberland and its commanding general were also exhausted from the battle's effects and the exertions of operating in mud and wet winter weather. Rosecrans's army had been simultaneously battered and pushed to the brink of annihilation like no other large Federal field army had in the war so far, and both it and its commander needed time to recover from such a near-death experience. On January 8, Rosecrans's command officially received the name Army of the Cumberland. The Right, Center and Left Wings became the XX, XIV and XXI Corps, respectively. All three corps commanders retained their positions.[114]

Meanwhile, Bragg reported his retreat to the Confederate government in Richmond. His announcement, coming on the heels of the cheering message of New Year's Eve, shocked the Confederacy. To the country, it appeared that Bragg had driven the Federals back and then retreated, as at Perryville. The Army of Tennessee's performance stood in sharp contrast to the Confederate armies in Virginia and Mississippi, each of which had won a major battle and held the battlefield afterward. The Southern press excoriated Bragg.[115]

Stung by the criticism, General Bragg now made a capital error that did as much as anything to destroy the Army of Tennessee's command climate. The army had barely settled into its winter camps when Bragg addressed this missive to his subordinates on January 11:

> *Finding myself assailed in private and public by the press, in private circles by officers and citizens, for the movement from Murfreesborough, which was resisted by me for some time after advised by my corps and division commanders, and only adopted after hearing of the enemy's re-enforcements*

by large numbers from Kentucky, it becomes necessary for me to save my fair name, if I cannot stop the deluge of abuse, which will destroy my usefulness and demoralize this army.

It has come to my knowledge that many of these accusations and insinuations are from staff officers of my generals, who persistently assert that the movement was made against the opinion and advice of their chiefs, and while the enemy was in full retreat. False or true, the soldiers have no means of judging me rightly or getting the facts, and the effect on them will be the same—a loss of confidence, and a consequent demoralization of the whole army. It is only through my generals that I can establish the facts as they exist. Unanimous as you were in council in verbally advising a retrograde movement, I cannot doubt that you will cheerfully attest the same in writing. I desire that you will consult your subordinate commanders and be candid with me, I have always endeavored to prove myself with you. If I have misunderstood your advice, and acted against your opinions, let me know it, in justice to yourself. If, on the contrary, I am the victim of unjust accusations, say so, and unite with me in staying the malignant slanders being propagated by men who have felt the sting of discipline.

General [Kirby] Smith has been called to Richmond, it is supposed, with a view to supersede me. I shall retire without a regret if I find I have lost the good opinion of my generals, upon whom I have ever relied as upon a foundation of rock.

Your early attention is most desirable, and is urgently solicited.

This message gives significant insight into Bragg's mindset and the strain on his fragile personality. It personalized the issue in a way that could not be undone and contained factual errors and accusations sure to arouse strong reactions. The penultimate paragraph was most unfortunate, for it unintentionally opened the door for a referendum on General Bragg's leadership. Even if Bragg survived such a confidence vote, he could never again command the same respect from his officers.[116]

The replies were not long in coming. The next day, Hardee, Breckinridge and Cleburne all responded individually. As requested, they had consulted their subordinates, including brigade leaders, thus spreading the command fissure deeper into the army's officer corps. The responses all agreed in substance with Hardee's letter:

I have the honor to acknowledge the receipt of your note of yesterday, in which, after informing me of the assaults to which you are subjected, you invoke a response in regard to the propriety of the recent retreat from Murfreesborough, and request me to consult my subordinate commanders in reference to the topics to which you refer. You will readily appreciate the delicate character of the inquiries you institute, but I feel, under the circumstances, that it is my duty to reply with the candor you solicit, not only from personal respect to yourself, but from the magnitude of the public interests involved.

In reference to the retreat, you state that the movement from Murfreesborough was resisted by you for some time, after advised by your corps and division commanders. No mention of retreat was made to me until early on the morning of the 3d of January, when Lieutenant Richmond, of General Polk's staff, read me the general's note to you, and informed me of your verbal reply. I told him, under the circumstances, nothing could be done then. About 10 o'clock the same day I met you personally at your quarters, in compliance with your request, Lieutenant-General Polk being present. You informed me that the papers of General McCook had been captured, and, from the strength of his corps (18,000), it appeared that the enemy was stronger than you had supposed; that General Wheeler reported he was receiving heavy re-enforcements, and, after informing us of these facts, suggested the necessity of retreat, and asked my opinion as to its propriety. Having heard your statements and views, I fully concurred, and it was decided to retreat. No preparation was made by me or my division commanders to retreat which was resisted by you for some time, and I recall your attention to the fact.

Afterward, in the evening, about 7 o'clock, we met to arrange details, and the retreat being still deemed advisable, and having been partially executed, I concurred in an immediate movement, in view of the heavy losses we had sustained, and the condition of the troops.

You also request me to consult my subordinate commanders, stating that General Smith has been called to Richmond, with the view, it was supposed, to supersede you, and that you will retire without regret, if you have lost the good opinion of your generals, upon whom you have ever relied as upon a foundation of rock. I have conferred with Major-General Breckinridge and Major-General Cleburne in regard to this matter, and I feel that frankness compels me to say that the general officers, whose judgment you have invoked, are unanimous in the opinion that a change in the command of this army is necessary. In this opinion I concur. I feel assured that this opinion is considerately formed, and with the highest respect for the purity of your motives, your energy, and your personal character; but they are convinced, as you must feel, that the peril of the country is superior to all personal considerations.

You state that the staff officers of your generals, joining in the public and private clamor, have, within your knowledge, persistently asserted that the retreat was made against the opinion and advice of their chiefs. I have made inquiries of the gentlemen associated with me, and they inform me that such statements have not been made or circulated by them.

General Polk was on leave from the army and did not respond until later in January. His subordinates felt that there was only one question to be answered, that of advising retreat, and they asked for clarification. Bragg seized this opportunity to halt the referendum. "To my mind that circular contained but one point of inquiry, and it certainly was intended to contain but one, and that was to ask of my corps and division commanders to commit to writing what had transpired between us in regard to the retreat from Murfreesborough," he replied. Polk, Cheatham and Withers all confirmed that they had advised retreat.[117]

Word of this exchange of notes reached President Davis in Richmond, and he ordered General Johnston to Tullahoma at once to investigate.

Joseph Johnston. *Library of Congress.*

"Why General Bragg should have selected that tribunal, and have invited its judgment upon him, is to me unexplained," the president fumed. Johnston arrived in Tullahoma on January 27 and interviewed Bragg and his principal subordinates. He found that Bragg had lost the confidence of most of his senior officers because of his conduct of both the Stones River battle and, more especially, the Kentucky Campaign. A tour of the camps showed, however, that the troops themselves remained in good spirits. Privately, Bragg wanted to be relieved of his position, but he apparently did not express his desires to Johnston. Bound by solicitation to Bragg's feelings and a sense of personal honor that would not allow him to advance at the expense of another, on February 3 Johnston endorsed Bragg's continuance in command.[118]

General Polk did not let the matter rest there, instead packaging all of the correspondence and sending it directly to President Davis in Richmond the next day. In a letter that sounded at best insubordinate and at worst mutinous, Polk lamented Bragg's "ill-judged" query and confirmed that his and his division commanders' views on Bragg as army commander "coincided with those of the other corps." He then went on to praise Bragg's "capacity for organization and discipline," suggesting that the general be transferred to staff duty in Richmond and replaced by General Johnston. "The state of this army demands immediate attention, and its position before the enemy, as well as the mind of its troops and commanders, could

Chattanooga as it appeared in April 1863. *National Archives.*

find relief in no way so readily as by the appointment of General Joseph E. Johnston," concluded Polk. Davis took no immediate action, and Johnston departed for Chattanooga.[119]

During the month of February, the Army of Tennessee's commanders filed their reports for Stones River, which they called the Battle of Murfreesboro. General Bragg could not resist the opportunity to strike back at his detractors. He challenged several of his subordinates' official reports, sometimes writing addenda or criticizing officers in his own report to shift blame. Breckinridge's report received special criticism in the form of a detailed sidebar from Bragg regarding the miscommunications and mismanagement of December 31. Bragg's own report was published in late February and made these attacks plain to the Confederacy, prompting several long rebuttals from his subordinates to the Confederate War Department during the months of March to June. As in the fall, turmoil in the army's high command had again spilled into the open.[120]

Davis decided to act and sent Johnston back to Tullahoma with a directive to take command and send Bragg to Richmond "for conference," orders that Johnston found personally distasteful. When Johnston arrived, he found that Mrs. Bragg had joined the army and lay sick. He refused to send the Braggs away while the general's wife was unwell and suspended their travel orders. By the time Mrs. Bragg recovered in early April, Johnston's Virginia wounds had flared and made him temporarily unfit for duty. For six weeks, the Army of Tennessee's top command was in limbo; Davis did not clarify who commanded the army, Bragg did not resign his position and Johnston held nominal command as senior officer present. Finally this farce ended in mid-April when Davis ordered the recovered Johnston to Mississippi, leaving Bragg in command.[121]

In this atmosphere, the army compiled the records covering the Kentucky Campaign. Polk and several of his subordinates had written and submitted their reports in November 1862, but Bragg did not prepare his report until May 20, 1863. He decided to assemble evidence and court-martial Polk for disobedience of orders at Bardstown on October 2 and at Perryville six days later. Bragg wrote to his officers (except Polk) on April 13 asking for details of a council of war in Bardstown, during which Polk decided to retreat instead of following Bragg's order to counterattack Buell's advance. The army commander also inquired about conferences on the morning of the Battle of Perryville that resulted in Polk not attacking, as Bragg intended. Several brigade and divisional generals responded to these questions, especially the pro-Bragg officers. Hardee declined to answer, citing the traditional confidentiality of such meetings. Hardee sent a copy of Bragg's request to Polk, adding, "If you choose to rip up the Kentucky campaign you can tear Bragg into tatters."[122]

Polk replied with a revealing letter on April 17:

> *I…thank you for the prompt indication of what was brewing. I am compelled to say it does not at all surprise me; so that when I said to you I felt it to be quite as necessary to watch Tullahoma as Murfreesborough you will see I was not mistaken in my estimate of the necessities of my position or of the character of others. As to the specific acts for which the arrest and trial are to be had (for I am satisfied that an arrest and trial are deliberately determined upon), I have to say I feel quite easy.*
>
> *…The report of the battle of Perryville which I sent to him [Bragg], and through him to the Senate beyond him, it is not allowable for him or any other person to use for public purposes until its contents have been publicly disclosed by order of the Senate to print. This is a trifle, but it belongs to the same family with that to which he invites attention. How far you may feel obliged for the protection he is affording you against the indiscretion or treachery by which you have been exposed, or whether that piece of service has won his way into your confidence far enough to lay you under obligations to join me in acknowledging disobedience to your duty, is a matter I am not competent to determine.*
>
> *I note what you say of the campaign. There is a time for all things, and I agree with you the time for dealing with that has not arrived.*

No charges were filed or court-martial convened. Nonetheless, these paper battles over the Kentucky expedition only widened the breaches in the Army of Tennessee's high command. Instead of planning and operating against the Army of the Cumberland, the Army of Tennessee's commanders in the spring of 1863 focused on waging a written war among themselves over past actions.[123]

This entire episode stands as an indictment of all involved. Bragg showed his erratic personality, alternately coming to his subordinates for help and also scheming against them. Despite privately wanting relief, Bragg did not force the issue by resigning his command in favor of General Johnston when the opportunity to do so presented itself. Johnston himself acted selfishly, twice failing to place the needs of his country above his notion of personal honor. Davis's failure to referee was dereliction of duty for the commander in chief of the Confederate armed forces—as a West Point graduate and former U.S. Army officer, Davis knew better and should have stepped in to resolve the situation. Both Hardee and especially Polk acted in a dishonest and mutinous manner, as antagonistic toward the headquarters behind them as the enemy in front.

The Army of Tennessee entered the summer of 1863 with a fractured command structure that destroyed any sense of teamwork needed to create and sustain a successful military organization. The deep fissures among the army's officers significantly hampered its ability to effectively operate during subsequent campaigns under Bragg's command. Those problems could have been rectified if Bragg or any of his superiors had acted decisively to straighten out the mess in the army's high command. Instead, the Army of Tennessee would fumble its last chance to hold Middle Tennessee. Primary responsibility for that calamity (and the subsequent failures in the fall of 1863) rested with Bragg, Johnston and Jefferson Davis.

Meanwhile, the war went on, as both armies faced each other and Rosecrans addressed problems of his own in the Army of the Cumberland.

Chapter 8
Murfreesboro Intermission

After Stones River, the scene of war shifted from Nashville proper to the areas south and southeast of the Tennessee capital. The Army of the Cumberland occupied Murfreesboro and spread detachments to other communities to grip Middle Tennessee. Two reconnaissances in mid-January ascertained Bragg's location and showed that poor weather and road conditions mandated a halt for the winter. Both armies settled into the quiet routine of winter quarters.[124]

The Federals received reinforcements, as Major General Gordon Granger had brought fourteen thousand men from Kentucky to join the Army of the Cumberland in January as its Reserve Corps. Granger himself was a stern and by-the-book type of soldier; Sheridan related that "his most serious failing was an uncontrollable propensity to interfere with and direct the minor matters relating to the command, the details for which those under him were alone responsible" and recalled his "freaky and spasmodic efforts to correct personally some trifling fault that ought to have been left to a regimental or company commander." Granger's corps camped around Franklin.[125]

While the Confederates fought among themselves in Tullahoma, Rosecrans refit his army. He rebuilt its strength by replacing his losses at Stones River in men and equipment. Brigadier General James Garfield replaced the deceased Garesche as chief of staff and improved the army's administrative apparatus. At first, Rosecrans's men consumed the three weeks' supplies built up in Nashville, while engineers struggled to repair the 212 miles of the L&N and Nashville & Chattanooga Railroads under U.S. control. On February 21, the first trains again made the trip from Louisville to Nashville and beyond. The rain and snow also raised the Cumberland's water level, allowing river traffic to Nashville.[126]

Rosecrans faced some turmoil in his army, mainly due to external politics. The largest issue in January concerned emancipation, for Lincoln's Emancipation Proclamation had freed all slaves in the rebellious states effective January 1, 1863. The proclamation specifically excluded all loyal states and territory under U.S. control on New Year's Day. Due to the press of operations in Kentucky and Tennessee, Rosecrans's soldiers had taken little notice of the preliminary announcement in September 1862 or the formal enactment, but now it excited much discussion in the camps. Most soldiers had enlisted to preserve the Union, while the army's Kentucky and Missouri units represented slave states. The officers of the 15th Kentucky vainly attempted to resign en masse in protest of the proclamation, but they were an exception. Most soldiers accepted the new war aim with some grumbling and pressed on.[127]

Another hot political issue concerned the growing peace movement in the United States. Known as Copperheads, many peaceniks had successfully run on Democratic tickets in the fall of 1862 and now took office. The Copperhead movement was strongest in Ohio, Indiana and Illinois, the three states that supplied most of the Army of the Cumberland's soldiers. Because of a lack of an absentee ballot system, few soldiers had voted, and many felt betrayed by their home politicians. During late winter and early spring, men from this army repeatedly and publicly wrote home stating their desire to keep fighting to preserve the Union. General Rosecrans himself weighed in on April 20: "This is war for the maintenance of the Constitution and its laws. I am amazed that anyone could think of peace on any terms. He who entertains the sentiment is fit only to be a slave; he who utters it at this time is a traitor to his country." Such sentiments prompted Radical Republicans in the North to quietly inquire about Rosecrans's interest in becoming secretary of war or president; the general was not interested.[128]

One of Rosecrans's biggest military headaches that spring was the need for more Union horsemen. The army had been deficient in cavalry since before Perryville, and the events of December again proved that the Army of the Cumberland needed more and better cavalry units to gather intelligence, screen the front against Confederate incursions and protect Union supply lines. Rosecrans continually requested tack and horses to remount his cavalry and sent back any deficient animals that were delivered. He also sought to equip his horsemen with repeating or breechloading rifles to gain a firepower edge over their Confederate counterparts. The general also approved Colonel John Wilder's request that his infantry brigade be mounted and given repeating rifles. Wilder's men spent the spring requisitioning horses and bought their seven-shot Spencer repeaters using a reimbursable subscription.[129]

These continual supply demands soon generated the ire of Washington, which in turn brought out one of Rosecrans's great failings: his periodic defensiveness and lack of tact. Halleck chided Rosecrans about his extensive telegraphing, prompting a sharp and thorough retort. To a suggestion from Quartermaster General Montgomery C. Meigs that he use wagons to transport his infantry so they could move faster, Rosecrans replied that it was a solution that "would do well on Pennsylvania Avenue," but not on Tennessee's rough roads. The worst outburst came when Halleck dangled a Regular Army major general's commission to the first army commander to win a major victory. Grant made no reply, but Rosecrans raged to Halleck that "I feel degraded to see such an auctioneering of honor." With his own subordinates he could be just as heated.[130]

Bragg faced logistical issues of his own at this time, namely the need to feed his men while camped in an area known as the Barrens. In late January, his army ran low on rations, and he appealed to both General Johnston and Commissary General Lucius Northrop in Richmond for help. Johnston and Bragg wanted to use the stocks of food in northern Georgia and Atlanta to meet the Army of Tennessee's needs. Northrop replied that those supplies were reserved for the Army of Northern Virginia, "and it alone. It is, and always has been, believed, and is still believed, by this bureau that the army…is in a country the resources of which are less exhausted than those tributary to the Army of [Northern] Virginia." Additional requests proved unavailing, forcing Bragg to forage far and wide for the needed sustenance. Supply remained a major headache for the Army of Tennessee all through the winter and spring. A visitor reported in April to President Davis: "The question of subsistence…is the vital one with this army…[T]he army is living hand to mouth, and drawing largely on the reserves."[131]

An additional, vexing problem that spring was the Confederate strategic situation. Johnston's Department of the West had been created to coordinate the operations of the Army of Tennessee with those of Lieutenant General John C. Pemberton's Army of Mississippi, located near Vicksburg, Mississippi. One of President Davis's ideas involved quickly shuttling troops back and forth to oppose Federal offensives; such a tactic had worked well in Virginia in May, June and July 1862. But Davis overlooked the fact that those troops operated no more than one hundred rail miles from one another, while transfers between Pemberton and Bragg covered six hundred miles of railroad. Stevenson's division had taken three weeks to get from Murfreesboro to Vicksburg in December; only two brigades arrived in time to help with the Confederate defense of that city, while that division's presence during the Stones River battle may well have tipped the balance in Bragg's favor.[132]

As department commander, Johnston struggled to solve this limitation of distance and time. He considered moving Bragg's army into Mississippi but demurred. Instead he formed a large cavalry corps under Major General Earl Van Dorn in southern Tennessee. Van Dorn had earned notoriety in the war by burning Grant's depot at Holly Springs, Mississippi, in December 1862, ending that officer's first attempt to take Vicksburg. Johnston wanted Van Dorn's command to aid Pemberton by harassing Federal forces in northern Mississippi and distracting Grant or to assist Bragg by raiding Rosecrans's supply lines. This plan proved only partially successful due to the poor winter weather and condition of the troopers.[133]

These logistical and strategic stresses, plus the strain of fighting among his officers, took a toll on General Bragg's health. In late May, Colonel Arthur J.L. Fremantle of the Coldstream Guards visited the Army of Tennessee while on a tour of the Confederacy. He described Bragg as "in appearance the least prepossessing of the Confederate generals. He is very thin; he stoops, and has a sickly, cadaverous, haggard appearance, rather plain features, bushy black eyebrows which unite in a tuft on the top of his nose, and a stubby iron-grey beard; but his eyes are bright and piercing." In Shelbyville, the colonel saw the first barefoot Confederate soldier on his trip. He described Liddell's brigade passing in review: "The men were good-sized, healthy, and well clothed, but without any attempt at uniformity in colour

Earl Van Dorn. *National Archives.*

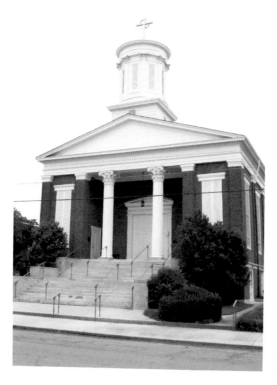

The First Presbyterian Church in Shelbyville, where Braxton Bragg was baptized on June 2, 1863. *Photograph by Terry R. Woodson.*

or cut; but nearly all were dressed either in grey or brown coats and felt hats." Fremantle also witnessed Bragg's baptism in Shelbyville on June 2.[134]

As winter turned to spring, flashes erupted between the armies as they brushed against each other. Almost daily skirmishes occurred along both armies' outpost lines. Rosecrans's efforts to garner more horsemen produced a cavalry corps of twelve thousand men in two divisions under General Stanley—the first time such a large Federal mounted force was constituted west of the Appalachian Mountains. Most of the men were green, but Stanley wanted to test his new command. Bragg had accumulated more than fifteen thousand horsemen under Wheeler's overall command and spread his front seventy miles from Columbia, Tennessee, into Kentucky to provision his men. Van Dorn commanded the force near Columbia with Forrest as his second in command, while John Hunt Morgan led the horsemen on Bragg's right. Confederate forage parties repeatedly searched to or behind Union lines for rations. Forrest and Wheeler raided the Federal supply line along the Cumberland River with limited success. As always, both sides sought information about the others' intentions.[135]

Joseph Wheeler. *Perryville Battlefield State Historic Site.*

By March, the roads had improved to allow more active operations, and both sides probed each other with cavalry over the next three months. The Confederates snuck behind Federal lines to snatch wagon trains and guards in hit-and-run operations. Meanwhile, Rosecrans and Stanley set about giving their horsemen experience against the Confederate cavalry, who up to this point in the war had proven markedly superior to their Federal counterparts. Basil Duke of Morgan's division summed up the Federal tactics:

> *Rosecrans was determined to make his superior numbers tell, at least, in the immediate vicinity of his army. He inaugurated a system, about this time, which resulted in the decided improvement of his cavalry. He would send out a body of cavalry, stronger than any thing it was likely to encounter, and that it might never be demoralized by a complete whipping, he would back it with an infantry force, never far in the rear, and always ready to finish the fight which the cavalry began. This method benefited the latter greatly.*

Against Morgan's troops, these methods proved quite successful; in a running battle at Liberty and Milton in March, a mixed Federal cavalry and infantry force inflicted serious casualties on Morgan's men, while in April some of Stanley's cavalry surprised Morgan's headquarters at McMinnville, narrowly failing to capture the general himself. By late April, General Morgan had moved most of his men into southern Kentucky to find forage and simply get out of the way.[136]

Over on the other flank, the Federals did not enjoy the same results against Van Dorn's more experienced and better-disciplined troopers. On March 4, an infantry brigade of 2,000 men under Colonel John Coburn marched south from Franklin to probe Van Dorn's positions. After skirmishing with Confederate outposts during the day, Coburn camped a few miles south of Franklin and pressed ahead the next morning. At 10:00 a.m. on March 5, he met Van Dorn's main body of 7,500 men deployed near Thompson's Station. After a short but sharp fight, most of Coburn's command was surrounded and forced to surrender. Against a loss of 357 casualties, the Confederates killed, wounded or captured 1,446 of the enemy. Forrest next raided the stockade at Brentwood on March 24, capturing 275 men and dozens of wagons; as he escaped southward, four Pennsylvania, Michigan and Kentucky cavalry regiments under Brigadier General Green Clay Smith caught up and recaptured some of the wagons and prisoners. Wheeler struck a blow in early April, penetrating to near the Hermitage and shelling the L&N railroad from across the Cumberland River.[137]

In April, Rosecrans planned some larger mounted expeditions. He proposed to send Stanley with a large body of cavalry, supported by Granger's infantry, south from Franklin to crush Van Dorn's corps. Neither general felt that it was a good idea; Stanley wrote his boss, "I do not know whether or not it would be judicious to attack with this green force, but if you think the 'game is worth the candle' we will slap at them." Rosecrans took the hint and canceled the operation.[138]

An operation that received sanction was a plan by Colonel Abel D. Streight to mount his infantry brigade and raid Bragg's supply line along the railroad between Chattanooga and Atlanta. Garfield pushed the plan onto a reluctant Rosecrans, who authorized the movement on April 7. Streight gathered his command of 1,700 men at Fort Donelson and moved via ship to Tuscumbia, Alabama, where he mounted all but 200 of his men. He set off on April 26, using a force under Brigadier General Grenville M. Dodge to unsuccessfully divert Van Dorn and Forrest's cavalry. The Federal raiders captured supplies, destroyed infrastructure, liberated slaves and pressed eastward through poor weather. Nonetheless, Forrest's determined pursuit finally caught Streight's exhausted command near Rome, Georgia. On May 3, the colonel and his men surrendered.[139]

In early May, the situation in Middle Tennessee shifted due to the war news from elsewhere. In Virginia, the Army of the Potomac's 125,000 men engaged the Army of Northern Virginia's 60,000 men in and around Chancellorsville and Fredericksburg; after ten days of marching and fighting, the Federals retreated across the Rappahannock. The armies had lost a total of 30,000 men, making the Battle of Chancellorsville the largest and bloodiest battle of the war to that point. Among the Confederate dead was national hero Lieutenant General Thomas J. "Stonewall" Jackson, a victim of friendly fire.[140]

In Mississippi, Grant spent much of April bringing his fleet down the river. On May 1, his army crossed at Bruinsburg,

Nathan Bedford Forrest. *National Archives.*

Mississippi, and in a lightning operation invested Vicksburg. This movement prompted the Confederate government in Richmond to strip Bragg's army of troops; three thousand of Van Dorn's horsemen rode into Mississippi, followed by Breckinridge's division by rail. Later, several more infantry brigades loaded at Tullahoma bound for Jackson, Mississippi.[141]

In Washington, Halleck prodded Rosecrans to advance. Each time, Rosecrans rebuffed him, even lecturing the general in chief about following the military maxim of not fighting two decisive battles simultaneously. Major General Ambrose E. Burnside had taken command of the forces in Kentucky, and in late May the two men worked out a plan for Burnside to push into East Tennessee while Rosecrans marched against Bragg's Tullahoma position. Halleck ironically short-circuited this movement by ordering the IX Corps, the heart of Burnside's army, to Mississippi as reinforcements for Grant.[142]

As Burnside dispatched his troops west, a political hot potato landed in Rosecrans's lap. Burnside had issued a strong sedition order in his department, and the nationally known Ohio Copperhead politician Clement L. Vallandigham had been arrested for criticizing the United States government. The Lincoln administration decided to expel him beyond Federal lines and sent Vallandigham to Murfreesboro. Rosecrans placed him under armed guard and vainly tried to transfer him to Bragg under flag of truce. After threatening Vallandigham with hanging if he ever returned, on May 26 Rosecrans sent the politician under escort to the picket line along the Shelbyville Road, where he was left with a letter that concluded, "Mr. Vallandigham is therefore handed over to the respectful attention of the Confederate authorities." After several awkward days in the Army of Tennessee's camps, Vallandigham was sent to North Carolina and thence to Bermuda.[143]

As the hot and dry weeks of May and early June 1863 passed, Halleck again queried Rosecrans about his plans. After the cancelation of the planned offensive with Burnside, Rosecrans polled his corps and division commanders about the propriety of an advance. Nearly all favored holding in place for the time being. These results were communicated to Halleck on June 11. "If you say that you are not prepared to fight Bragg I shall not order you to do so, for the responsibility of fighting or refusing to fight at a particular time and place must rest upon the general in immediate command," replied Halleck the next day.[144]

Washington may not have been able to see it, but the Army of the Cumberland was preparing for an advance from Murfreesboro. Federal spies inside Bragg's lines gave Rosecrans a good indication of the terrain and Confederate dispositions opposite. Wary of again losing his communications during a campaign, Rosecrans built up a substantial supply reserve in Murfreesboro and Nashville. He also ordered his men to take twelve days' rations with them when the army advanced. To protect his base at Murfreesboro, Rosecrans built a massive two-hundred-acre earthen fortification outside town that became known as Fortress Rosecrans. Stocked with heavy artillery and plenty of rations and ammunition, Fortress Rosecrans could withstand a major siege.[145]

Pressure built from Washington for an offensive. On June 16, Halleck inquired, "Is it your intention to make an immediate movement forward? A definite answer, yes or no, is required." That evening, Rosecrans answered, "If immediate means tonight or tomorrow, no. If it means as soon as all things are ready, say five days, yes."[146]

One week later, General Rosecrans was ready. At 2:10 a.m. on June 24, he sent the telegram that Halleck had been waiting for: "The army begins to move at 3 o'clock this morning." After 169 days of rest, the Army of the Cumberland was again on the march.[147]

Chapter 9

Into the Mountains

The operation that started on June 24, 1863, became known as the Tullahoma Campaign or the Middle Tennessee Campaign. As it commenced, momentous events occurred in other theaters. In the East, Lee's Army of Northern Virginia completed its crossing of the Potomac River and moved its lead elements into Pennsylvania. Along the Mississippi River, two Federal armies locked two Confederate armies in sieges at the critical bastions of Vicksburg, Mississippi, and Port Hudson, Louisiana. All four operations climaxed during the first ten days of July 1863, collectively marking a key turning point in the Civil War.

The Tullahoma Campaign occurred in one of the wilder and latest-settled areas in Tennessee. Three main roads radiated from Murfreesboro, running east to Bradyville, southeast to Manchester and south to Shelbyville. Fifteen miles out from Murfreesboro stretched the Highland Rim, a line of steep hills that shielded the Army of Tennessee. The Highland Rim loomed 500 to 900 feet above Murfreesboro and was broken by several gaps. The three main defiles separating the two armies were Hoover's Gap on the Manchester Pike, Liberty Gap north of Bell Buckle and Guy's Gap north of Shelbyville. Behind the Highland Rim stood a forty-mile-wide area known as the Barrens, a flat and sandy area of cattle and horse farms. The Barrens were bounded by Shelbyville to the west, Manchester to the northeast and Winchester to the southeast. The Elk and Duck Rivers bisected the area, crossing any line of march to the southeast. The N&C Railroad had been cut through the Barrens in the early 1850s, giving rise to small towns (Bell Buckle, Wartrace, Tullahoma, Estill Springs, Decherd and Cowan) at various points along the line. East of Cowan loomed the mighty Cumberland Plateau, a forbidding mountain range blocking Chattanooga. A 2,228-foot-long tunnel outside Cowan was a critical logistical link in the railroad.[148]

Confederate infantry and cavalry defended all of the major routes leading out of Murfreesboro. During the winter, Bragg had reorganized the Army of Tennessee and kept it arrayed along the Highland Rim to watch the Federals. His army totaled an effective strength of 43,000 men.[149] Polk's Corps of 14,000 men occupied its winter quarters around Shelbyville, which had been fortified. Major Generals Cheatham and Withers remained in command of Polk's divisions. General Hardee headquartered at Wartrace, spreading his 15,000 men behind Hoover's and Liberty Gaps. Cleburne's division camped near Bell Buckle on the left, while newly promoted Major General A.P. Stewart held the area around Fairfield with a division composed of the parts of McCown's and Breckinridge's divisions not sent to Mississippi. A thin line of cavalry and infantry pickets covered the Highland Rim's gaps. Confederate cavalry guarded the army's flanks, with Wheeler's 9,000-man cavalry corps posted along the Highland Rim. On May 7, General Van Dorn had been murdered by a man who caught the general having an affair with his wife; the 4,000 horsemen left at Spring Hill and Columbia after the detachments to Mississippi now fell under Forrest's command. John Hunt Morgan patrolled Bragg's right with his division of 2,500 men. On June 20, he set off into Kentucky on an ambitious operation aimed at penetrating north of the Ohio River. The Federals detected his departure, and Rosecrans warned Burnside of trouble coming to the Bluegrass State.[150]

Rosecrans faced several options as he sought to attack the Army of Tennessee. He could march south against Shelbyville and Spring Hill, cutting Bragg's forage supply. Another option was to make a wide turning movement through McMinnville against Tullahoma. However, both of these routes would take Rosecrans away from his overall objective of Chattanooga, create supply problems by being away from the railroad and give Bragg an opening to strike the Army of the Cumberland's flank and rear. Rosecrans instead chose to challenge Bragg directly along the Highland Rim. The general later explained his plan:

Positive information from various sources concurred to show the enemy intended to fight us in his intrenchments at Shelbyville, should we advance by that route, and that he would be in good position to retreat if beaten, and so retard our pursuit through the narrow, winding roads from that place which lead up to The Barrens, and thus inflict severe loss without danger to their own line of retreat to the mountains toward their base. I was determined to render useless their intrenchments, and, if possible, secure their line of retreat by turning their right and moving on the railroad bridge across Elk River. This would compel a battle on our own ground or drive them on a disadvantageous line of retreat. To accomplish this it was necessary to make Bragg believe we could advance on him by the Shelbyville route, and to keep up the impression, if possible, until we had reached Manchester with the main body of the army.

Rosecrans did not meet with his subordinates to explain the operation, instead preferring to issue daily orders to his corps commanders via telegraph or courier. He evidently expected a fast-moving campaign that might require quick changes of plan under his personal observation.[151]

The Army of the Cumberland entered this campaign with five corps totaling seventy thousand men. Thirteen thousand of Granger's troops stayed behind to guard Nashville and other key points in Middle Tennessee, while Van Cleve's XXI Corps division garrisoned Murfreesboro. Crittenden's XXI Corps moved toward Bradyville with ten thousand infantrymen and a cavalry force under Brigadier General John V. Turchin, while Thomas's XIV Corps of twenty-six thousand men marched on the direct road to Manchester. McCook's sixteen thousand XX Corps soldiers feinted toward the Highland Rim gaps near Shelbyville, while seven thousand men of Granger's Reserve Corps and most of Stanley's Cavalry Corps of twelve thousand horsemen guarded the Federal right flank and watched Forrest.[152]

Rosecrans's columns marched out from Murfreesboro at 7:00 a.m. on June 24. That morning, the dry weather broke. A steady rain fell fourteen of the next seventeen days, almost daily from June 24 through July 7, hampering the movements of both sides. Oppressive heat and humidity cloaked the Barrens between rainstorms. "The roads seem to have been lost, as we passed through woods with bottomless mud," wrote Hazen.[153]

Thomas's XIV Corps made the first enemy contact along the macadamized Manchester Pike. Reynolds's division led the march, followed by the divisions of Rousseau and Negley. Brigadier General John M. Brannan's division lingered to the rear to support McCook and Granger. Wilder's mounted infantry brigade rode at the front of the column with orders to secure the entrance to Hoover's Gap. General Stanley had derided this brigade as "tadpole cavalry," and Wilder felt the need to prove his men's prowess in battle.[154]

The 1st Kentucky Cavalry (C.S.) stood on picket north of Hoover's Gap. Its mission was to provide warning of a Federal movement and delay the enemy long enough for Confederate infantry to occupy the powerful earthworks at Hoover's Gap itself. Two infantry brigades under Bushrod Johnson and

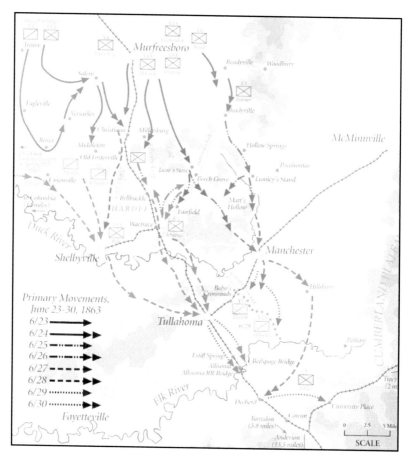

The Tullahoma Campaign. *Courtesy Greg Biggs.*

Brigadier General William B. Bate camped four miles away near Fairfield, a 90- to 120-minute march from the gap. This defense plan depended on good staff work and coordination to be successful, but both of these were in short supply given the current command climate in the Army of Tennessee. Troops were also hard to come by; Hardee had earlier complained about his line being too long for the force at hand.[155]

Wilder's horsemen encountered the Confederate Kentuckians seven miles out from Murfreesboro. The Federals skirmished with them while waiting for Reynolds's infantry to arrive. Once the division caught up, Wilder put his men in column with the 72nd Indiana and elements of the 17th Indiana out front and on the flanks for protection and started a running fight with the Confederate cavalry for eight miles. By midday, the Kentuckians had fled to Hoover's Gap with Wilder's soldiers on their heels. Sensing the opportunity for a *coup de main*, Wilder pointed his men into the gap itself. "I directed the advance to push speedily forward and take possession of Hoover's Gap, and, if possible, to prevent the enemy from occupying their fortifications," he reported.[156]

Wilder's Indianans and Illinoisans rushed forward with a will, scattering the Kentuckians and capturing their battle flag. As the 1st Kentucky collapsed, the Federals entered the gap and beheld the rolling terrain beyond, bisected by the Garrison Fork of the Duck River. Prisoners confirmed the presence of Stewart's infantry at Fairfield. "I determined to take the entire gap," recalled Wilder, "and, if possible, hold it until the arrival of the infantry column, now some 6 miles behind us, believing that it would cost us at least a thousand men to retake the ground we now held, if it was reasonably contested by the rebel force close at hand. My whole command was rapidly moved forward to the southern extremity of the gap, and while being placed in position we heard the long-roll sounded in the rebel camp at our right, 2 miles down the Garrison Fork." His men took position at Hoover's Gap's southern entrance and pushed patrols forward to reconnoiter.[157]

In Fairfield, the situation was confused, as the unexpected arrival of disorganized cavalry spread an alarm through Bate's and Johnson's brigades. Johnson's command, camped farther south than Bate's brigade, appeared to get the news first, for Bate only started reacting after Stewart ordered him to move toward the gap. "The Yanks had run over our cavalry, and came very near surprising us," recalled a captain in the 20th Tennessee of Bate's brigade.[158]

Bate's Tennessee and Georgia troops pushed toward Hoover's Gap, skirmishing with Wilder's pickets. In the middle of the afternoon, they encountered the main Federal line of resistance along a ridge blocking the gap's southern entrance. Wilder's five regiments were supported by Captain Eli Lilly's 18th Indiana Battery. Bate spent time probing the line and bringing up the rest of his men. Confederate artillery dueled with Lilly's guns. In the late afternoon, Bate launched a disjointed series of attacks against all parts of the Federal position, forcing Wilder to shift his men around to respond. The Federal Spencer rifles gave the defenders a marked advantage. "We went at it shooting," recalled an Indianan, "and…we got them to running, which is one of the nicest sights I have seen." Lilly's battery anchored the defense, suppressing some of Bate's artillery and helping repel the charges. Bate's efforts to flank the Federals were repelled by what Wilder called "our leaden hail." The frustrated Confederates pulled back, having lost 25 percent of their number. Wilder's Federals lost sixty-one dead and wounded.[159]

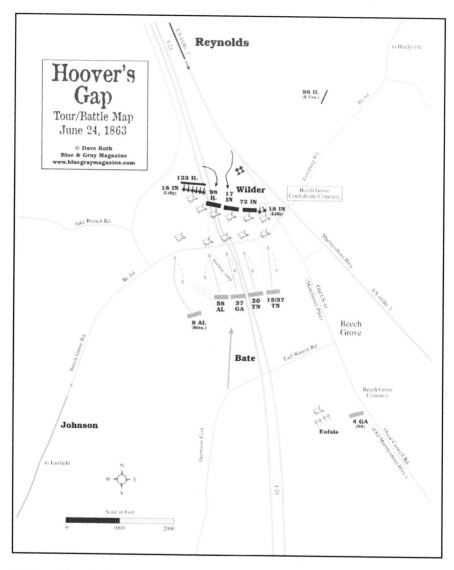

Action at Hoover's Gap, June 24. *Map by David Roth.*

In the evening, both sides received reinforcements. As dusk fell, General Stewart arrived in person and relieved Bate's troops with Bushrod Johnson's Tennesseans. Reynolds's Federal infantry took up position south of the gap, supported by elements of Rousseau's division. Generals Rosecrans and Thomas also visited Hoover's Gap that evening. The usually reserved Thomas gushed to Colonel Wilder, "You have saved the lives of a thousand

Hoover's Gap as it looks in 2011, looking north from about the Confederate line on June 24–26. Interstate 24 and the interchange for Exit 97 obliterated most of the ridge defended by Wilder's Federals. The towers mark the approximate width of the Lightning Brigade's front. *Photograph by Terry R. Woodson.*

men by your gallant conduct today. I didn't expect to get this gap for three days." The next day, Thomas decreed that Wilder's unit would henceforth be known as the Lightning Brigade, in recognition of its quick and decisive actions on June 24.[160]

Farther to the west, McCook's XX Corps left Murfreesboro about 8:00 a.m. The lead division under Richard Johnson met resistance from Confederate cavalry along the road to Liberty Gap, where the Liberty Pike crosses the Highland Rim. Detachments from General Liddell's Arkansas brigade held this pass, while the rest of Liddell's infantry camped three miles rearward around Bell Buckle. Unlike Hoover's Gap, Liberty Gap actually had two passes: Liberty Gap itself, a quarter-mile-long gorge that opened into a four-square-mile valley, and an unnamed inner defile on the valley's south end. The Confederates picketed the outer gap with their camps in the valley's north end.[161]

Richard Johnson's advance started in the late morning as General Willich's brigade pushed toward the outer gap using the 39th Indiana Mounted Infantry as a screen. Recalled Willich:

On my advance, the enemy's skirmishers fell back on their reserves, which were posted on the crest of the hills forming the northern entrance of Liberty Gap. There the enemy had a very strong, and, in front, easily defended position. The hills are steep, to half their heights open, then rocky and covered with woods. I felt the enemy in front to ascertain whether he would make a decided resistance, and found him in force and determined.

He paused to extend his lines and find the Confederate flanks.[162]

Meanwhile, the Confederates—540 men of the 5th and 13th/15th Arkansas—quickly deployed along the heights and prepared to make a stand. Both regimental commanders, Colonels Lucius Featherson of the 5th and John E. Josey of the 13th/15th, were caught by surprise, having expected to receive warning from Confederate cavalry pickets in their front. "The enemy surprised this invincible cavalry, and…was within 600 yards of Liberty Gap before Colonel Featherston or myself knew of the advance," recalled Colonel Josey. Featherston left his lunch to enter the battle. Informing General Liddell of the Federal push, Featherston put the

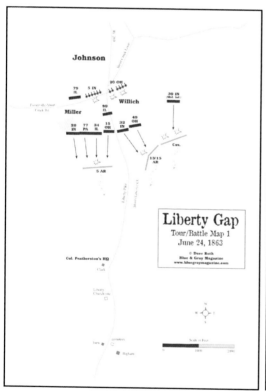
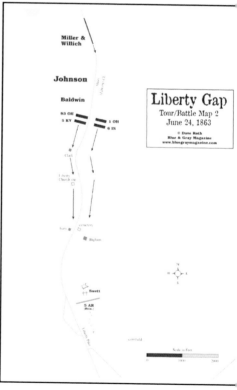

Action at Liberty Gap, June 24. *Maps by David Roth.*

Liberty Gap in 2011, as seen from the Federal artillery positions looking south. The Confederates defended the high ground in the distance on June 24. *Photograph by Terry R. Woodson.*

Chockley's Tavern in Wartrace served as Cleburne's headquarters. This picture was taken in 2011. *Photograph by Terry R. Woodson.*

two regiments in position along the outer gap, where they traded fire with Willich's Federals. The 5th defended the left of the road, while the 13th/15th held the right. Colonel Josey described how his men spent several hours that afternoon "fighting hard all the time and at short range."[163]

Richard Johnson called up more troops, and the Federal superiority in numbers soon had an effect. The 39th Indiana found a defile to the east near the railroad passage over the Highland Rim and rode toward the flank and rear of the 13th/15th Arkansas. At the same time, Willich sent the 49th Ohio and parts of the 32nd Indiana against the front of the gap. These men, "under a murderous fire, drove the enemy before them," recalled Willich. Liddell ordered the two regiments back to the south end of the valley, where he posted the rest of his brigade. Featherston initially refused to retire because of "my men being well secured, and doing full execution." Willich's Federals nonetheless pushed through Liberty Gap, capturing Featherston's regimental camp and his table still set for lunch. By 5:00 p.m., the Confederates stood in their new line along the inner gap, leaving the rest of the area to the Federals. That evening, Johnson's and Davis's Federal divisions moved into the vacated Confederate positions around the outer gap.[164]

Thomas J. Wood. *Perryville Battlefield State Historic Site.*

While the other corps fought on the 24th to gain passage through the gaps, Crittenden's XXI Corps marched to Bradyville and struggled to ascend Gillies' Hill east of town. General Wood had reduced his divisional baggage to a minimum, but General Palmer had not; Palmer's numerous wagons churned the road into "mud and mire," according to Wood. Infantry worked day and night to help push wagons and artillery through the knee-deep mud and up the slopes, a time-consuming and exhaustive process. "Horses and mules, floundering in the mud, were unhitched, and artillery and ammunition wagons dragged through deep morasses by the infantry," recalled Lieutenant Colonel Gilbert C. Kniffin. "In some places mules perished in the mud, unable to extricate themselves." Palmer's division took two and a half days to climb Gillies' Hill, not completing the ascent until noon on June 27. Wood's division followed over the next eleven hours, and Crittenden's troops finally all reached Manchester on June 28. The XXI Corps took four full days to travel the thirty-five miles from Murfreesboro to Manchester via Bradyville, a distance that normally should have taken two or three days. When Crittenden's men arrived, they were exhausted and not ready for battle. "But for the heavy rains Crittenden would have joined McCook and Thomas two days earlier, and the campaign might have had a different ending," lamented Kniffin.[165]

On the night of June 24, Rosecrans considered the situation and issued his orders for the next day. Despite the rain, the day had been a good one for the Army of the Cumberland. In sharp fighting, the Federals had managed to thrust aside the Army of Tennessee's shield along the Highland Rim. Thomas's corps obtained a secure lodgment at Hoover's Gap, while McCook's men met their objectives by forcing Liberty Gap. On the Federal right, Polk and Forrest remained quiet. Concerned about a possible surge from Guy's Gap or counterattack against Thomas, Rosecrans decided to consolidate before pushing farther. "Look carefully to your right flank," he admonished McCook.[166]

June 25 opened rainy. At Liberty Gap, McCook's Federals faced Liddell's Confederates in the valley. "A desultory fire was kept up between the forces on outpost along the entire front, at long range, and with but few, if any casualties," recalled an Illinoisan. Sheridan's division arrived and camped beyond the outer gap in reserve. At 3:00 p.m., McCook ordered his supply trains shifted north to the Manchester Pike, in preparation for the rest of the XX Corps to follow the next day.[167]

From his position at the inner gap, General Liddell perceived some of these movements and decided to probe the Federal line. At 4:00 p.m., the Confederates attacked into the valley with two regiments. Willich's skirmishers gave way, but a countercharge by the 49th Ohio pushed back the Confederates. Reinforcements under Colonel John Miller arrived to stabilize the line. Miller lost his left eye shot out, and his brigade wavered just as Liddell committed more infantry into another attack. Carlin's infantry brigade of Davis's division counterattacked, pushing Liddell's Arkansans back to the inner gap. Late in the fighting, the 2nd Arkansas held a ledge along the inner gap against Carlin's Federals. "We were stationed at the side

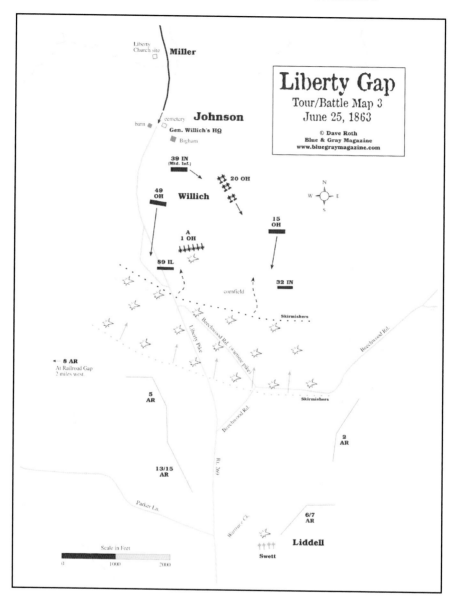

This page and next: Action at Liberty Gap, June 25. *Maps by David Roth.*

of a steep, rocky hill, and when our color bearer was killed he fell down the hill into the Federal lines, and they got our flag," recalled a member of that unit. The 38th Illinois picked up the colors. As dusk fell, Liddell's men pulled back into the inner gap, leaving McCook's Federals in control of the valley.[168]

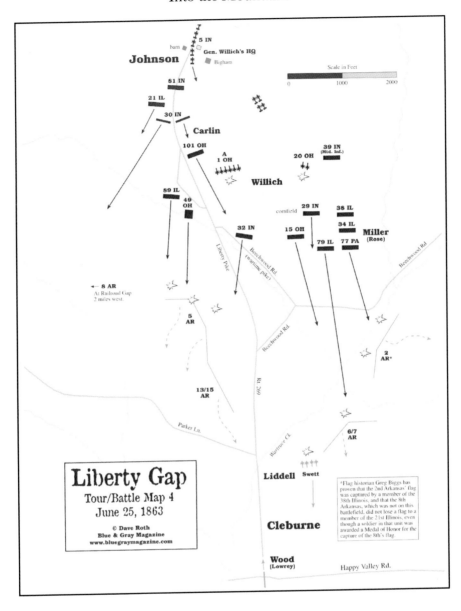

Liberty Gap
Tour/Battle Map 4
June 25, 1863

© Dave Roth
Blue & Gray Magazine
www.bluegraymagazine.com

Over at Hoover's Gap, General Thomas's XIV Corps held position on June 25 and prepared to break out to the south and southeast. The Federals planned to drive the Confederates toward Fairfield and away from the Manchester Pike. Five miles southeast of Hoover's Gap, the pike entered Matt's Hollow, a mile-long narrow defile that drew comparisons to the pass at Thermopylae. General Thomas was anxious to capture Matt's Hollow

The June 25 battlefield at Liberty Gap, looking from the Confederate approach. The Federals held the tree-studded rise in the middle distance. *Photograph by Terry R. Woodson.*

without a fight. The rain delayed the XIV Corps' deployments until late in the day, and the offensive was postponed until the next morning. Meanwhile Bushrod Johnson's Confederates harassed the Federals with shellfire, sniping and skirmishing.[169]

As night fell on June 25, Rosecrans issued orders for a renewed advance on June 26 and 27. Expecting Bragg to remain quiet, Rosecrans directed McCook to leave Davis's division at Liberty Gap, taking Sheridan's and Richard Johnson's divisions north to the Manchester Pike. Thomas's XIV Corps received orders to break out and move toward Manchester, pushing Stewart's Confederates toward Fairfield while the Lightning Brigade secured Matt's Hollow. Crittenden's two divisions, still struggling up Gillies' Hill, were directed toward Manchester to join the XIV Corps there. The Federal plan to turn Bragg's right was working, despite the weather.[170]

As these orders went out, Rosecrans could feel confident. But Bragg had finally been aroused to action.

Chapter 10
Tullahoma Maneuvers

The Army of the Cumberland's advance had caught the Army of Tennessee flat-footed. The Confederate response so far had been passive and generally uncoordinated. Bragg's cavalry failed to give adequate warning, and the XIV Corps forced its way through Hoover's Gap. Cleburne's men held Liberty Gap, but it appeared that they faced a superior force that could push through at any time. To complicate matters, most of the Confederate cavalry was stationed on the Army of Tennessee's western flank and away from the Federal main effort, making timely intelligence about the enemy's movements hard to obtain. On the evening of June 25, Bragg ordered some cavalry to ride from west of Shelbyville to Manchester to help screen the eastern flank.[171]

Rosecrans was not about to give Bragg time to react if he could help it. Thomas's breakout from Hoover's Gap started shortly after 10:30 a.m. on June 26. Bate's and Bushrod Johnson's infantry stood astride a ridge that straddled both the Manchester Pike and the Fairfield Road. Most of their strength was concentrated on the Confederate left, along the Fairfield Road, in compliance with orders from Hardee to retire toward Fairfield and Wartrace if attacked. Thomas planned for Reynolds's infantry to attack the Confederate right, while Rousseau's and Brannon's divisions hit the Confederate center and left. Meanwhile, the Lightning Brigade received orders to take Matt's Hollow. Reynolds would follow with his infantry.[172]

After an artillery duel, Thomas's infantry moved forward. Wilder's brigade quickly cleared the Manchester Pike and rode southeast, securing Matt's Hollow without opposition in the afternoon. Thomas's main infantry attack bogged down in front of Bushrod Johnson's Tennesseans for a time. A charge

Above: The Hoover's Gap battlefield, viewed from the Confederate position along the Manchester Pike. Thomas's Federals attacked from the right side of the picture and evicted Bushrod Johnson's Confederates from the far ridge on June 26. This photograph was taken in 2011 in similar weather conditions. *Photograph by Terry R. Woodson.*

Left: Matt's Hollow as seen in 2011. *Photograph by Terry R. Woodson.*

by the Regular Brigade and Brigadier General Moses B. Walker's brigade finally cracked the Confederate line, and other Federal units swarmed Johnson's position. Close-quarters fighting raged along the ridge. "Some of the rebs tried to use their bayonet, but the most of them turned and run up hill; others threw down their rifles in token of surrender. We speedily followed up hill in pursuit but it was hard work, the ridge was so steep," recalled Lieutenant John H. Otto of the 21st Wisconsin. "The enemy fled with precipitation towards Fairfield," reported General Rousseau. Stewart rallied his command around Fairfield and prepared a defense. The divisions of Brannan and Rousseau followed but made no attack.[173]

Meanwhile, in the early afternoon, Bragg met with General Polk in Shelbyville to discuss a response to the Federal offensive. Feeling aggressive, Bragg proposed that Polk march his corps through Guy's Gap during the night, turn east and make a dawn attack on June 27 against the Federal troops around Liberty Gap. Cleburne's troops would support the movement with an assault from Liberty Gap's south side. Little information was available about Federal strength or dispositions, so Polk's fourteen thousand infantry would essentially be pushing into a void with no cavalry to protect the flanks or provide information. "Owing to the character of the country, the heavy cedar growth, and the peculiar topography, the general [Polk] objected, considering the position he was about being thrown in nothing short of a man-trap," recalled Polk's aide-de-camp, Lieutenant W.B. Richmond. Bragg overrode these objections and directed Polk to make the offensive.[174]

Later that afternoon, word of Stewart's defeat at Hoover's Gap arrived in Shelbyville. Realizing the implications of being driven off the Manchester Pike, General Bragg changed his mind about a counterstrike. "Movement proposed for tomorrow is abandoned," he wrote to Polk at 4:00 p.m.[175]

The aborted Guy's Gap operation has since engendered some discussion and is one of the greater what-ifs in the Army of Tennessee's career. Bragg's aggressiveness is commendable; indeed, Rosecrans had expected just such a move on June 25. Had Polk carried out the march as ordered, he would have encountered the five thousand men of Davis's Federal division at Liberty Gap, plus fourteen thousand infantry and cavalry under Granger and Stanley near Christiana, in position to strike Polk's flank and rear. It would have been a tall order for Polk's infantry to defeat all these units, but had they done so it might have wrecked Rosecrans's campaign and forced him to retire to Murfreesboro to protect his supplies. However, any Confederate exploitation toward Murfreesboro would have faced the weather, poor roads, Federal rear-guard detachments and Van Cleve's infantry ensconced

A 2011 view of the Highland Rim along the Murfreesboro-Shelbyville Road. Guy's Gap is the notch in the left center. *Photograph by Terry R. Woodson.*

in Fortress Rosecrans. Polk may have been right to object, but he helped toss away the best chance in the campaign for a counterstrike.[176]

A more fruitful use of Polk's troops would have been to march them the fourteen miles to Fairfield for a morning attack on June 27 toward Hoover's Gap and the Manchester Pike. Combined with Stewart's division, Polk's Confederates would have outnumbered Rousseau's and Brannan's Federals and could have pushed them back to Hoover's Gap. Choking off that road and pass would have cut Rosecrans's army in two, with Thomas's XIV Corps and Crittenden's XXI Corps separated from McCook's, Granger's and Stanley's Federals. Such a development would have short-circuited Rosecrans's operations, forcing him to withdraw via Bradyville or turn around and fight his way back through Hoover's Gap to save the isolated portion of his army. There is no record that Bragg, Polk or Hardee ever considered this option.

Had Bragg paused to reflect, he may have realized that the bitter seeds of the spring had now ripened. His written war with his generals had destroyed communication, teamwork and coordination among the Army of Tennessee's senior echelons. Communication and coordination failures played a role in the reverses at Hoover's and Liberty Gaps and helped keep Bragg as army commander in the dark during the first crucial days of Rosecrans's advance. Perhaps most importantly, the discord in the army's high command had prevented detailed contingency planning for defending against a Federal advance; had Bragg, Polk, Hardee and the other commanders been functioning as a proper team, countermeasures like the Guy's Gap strike would have been thoroughly discussed, planned and decided before the campaign even began. These plans in hand, the Army of Tennessee would have immediately executed a coordinated response to the Federal moves. Instead, Bragg struggled to cobble together a major counteroffensive under a general he hated in the midst of a fluid and uncertain situation.[177]

The decision to abandon the Guy's Gap operation took the resolution out of General Bragg; an hour after calling off the offensive, he queried Polk about whether the army should "hold a line this side of Tullahoma, to strike the enemy successfully this side of Tullahoma, or is a retreat to Tullahoma a necessity?" That night, Bragg answered his own question, ordering his entire army to retreat.[178]

Early on June 27, the Army of Tennessee began the wet and slow slog to Tullahoma. Wheeler's cavalry covered the retreat, while Forrest's corps rode east to join the army. Polk's Corps started evacuating Shelbyville at 5:30 a.m., the rear units not departing until 8:00 a.m. The bishop's troops marched all day via Rowesville on the direct Shelbyville-Tullahoma Road eighteen miles to Tullahoma. Stewart's division fell back six miles to Wartrace and then moved via Normandy to Tullahoma, a distance of about nineteen miles, which also took all day. Cleburne's command started falling back to Wartrace, his last elements not leaving Bell Buckle until the next morning.[179]

The march was not without its problems, however. Due to a staff mix-up, Cleburne's troops were ordered southwest from Wartrace to Rowesville and the Tullahoma Road, instead of following Stewart's route southeast via Normandy. As a result, his men "cut into line," according to Lieutenant Richmond, and were halted "until the whole of Cheatham's division had passed." Firing from rearguard skirmishes at Wartrace and Shelbyville punctuated the muddy traffic jam. It was not until after dark that the head of Cleburne's command finally got moving, but it ran into a further delay caused by Colonel D.M. Donnell of the 16th Tennessee, who interpreted his orders strictly that no wagons be left behind. "Colonel Donnell, for one, stops his command, and, in consequence, everything in rear of him, whenever a wagon breaks down," complained Cleburne. At 10:00 p.m., Bragg's headquarters directed that wrecked wagons be shoved out of the way so that Cleburne's men could complete their march.[180]

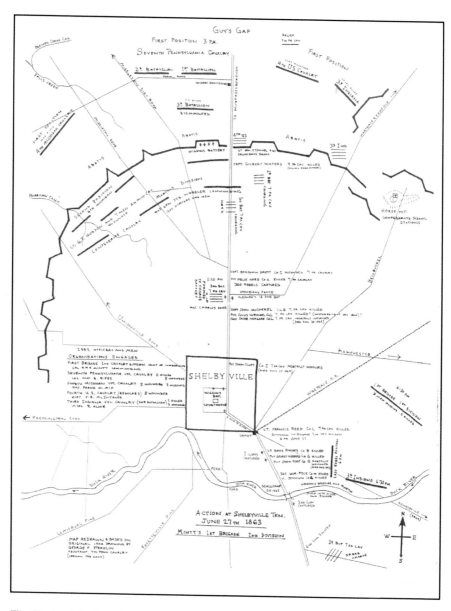

The Battle of Shelbyville. *Courtesy Greg Biggs.*

The Federal army posed the biggest problem to the Army of Tennessee on June 27, as Stanley's cavalry pressured the Confederate rear. At 8:00 a.m., Stanley probed Guy's Gap with his corps, skirmishing with Colonel

Robert H.G. Minty's cavalry brigade as elements of Brigadier General Robert B. Mitchell's cavalry division flanked the gap to the east. After a two-hour skirmish, Minty's troopers charged through the Confederate roadblock and pursued the Confederates seven miles to Shelbyville. General Wheeler made a stand in the town's fortifications with 1,200 Confederate horsemen of Brigadier General William T. Martin's division. The rain-swollen Duck River flowed east–west one mile south of town. Wheeler had to hold, for Forrest was less than ten miles away and riding hard to try and cross the Duck at Shelbyville.[181]

Minty rode forward with his brigade, composed of 2,200 men of the 1st Middle Tennessee, 3rd Indiana, 4th Michigan, 4th U.S. and 7th Pennsylvania Cavalry Regiments. They approached from the north along the Murfreesboro Road, encountering the Confederate works on a small rise three miles from the courthouse square. The Murfreesboro Road ran southward into town to the square, where it fanned out in several directions. Minty sent the 4th Michigan Cavalry to the right and the 3rd Indiana Cavalry to the left of the road to develop the situation, supporting the Indianans with the 4th U.S. Cavalry. The Indianans got lost in the undergrowth, wandering eastward to the Bell Buckle and Fairfield Roads. They turned and pushed toward Shelbyville from the east.[182]

Meanwhile, the Michiganders and Regulars skirmished with Wheeler's men along the Murfreesboro Road. Minty arrayed the 7th Pennsylvania Cavalry in column along the road with sabers drawn. Judging his moment, about 4:00 p.m. Minty ordered his men to charge. Lieutenant Colonel Robert Sipe signaled his Pennsylvanians to advance and related what happened next:

> With the main body of the regiment, I went up the road, closing well upon the advance, and immediately engaged the rebel force. Leaving the road, which was covered by other regiments rapidly coming up, I went to the left, and instructed my force to pursue the enemy through the woods, where they were flying thick and fast. This movement proved very successful, my men having crowded a large number of the enemy into a field surrounded by a picket fence, where they captured them ad libitum. The effect of this charge in detail was most disastrous to the rebels. Many were killed and wounded. The number of prisoners taken was almost equal to the force I had engaged, and the field was literally strewn with arms, clothing, blankets, &c.

Within minutes Wheeler's command lost more than three hundred prisoners and reeled back into town in disorder.[183]

The Bedford County Courthouse in downtown Shelbyville, as seen in 2011. *Photograph by Terry R. Woodson.*

The 7th Pennsylvania Cavalry charged up this road to break Wheeler's last stand in Shelbyville, 2011 view. *Photograph by Terry R. Woodson.*

General Wheeler formed a line at the courthouse, using his four cannons to anchor the defense. He sought a way out, but the Indianans had closed the way east to Rowesville. The only other route to safety was to the southeast via the Skullcamp Bridge. Wheeler needed to hold until dark so his men could use the night to cover their escape.[184]

Minty's men reformed and sent their prisoners to the rear. The colonel himself sought to give the enemy no break. He sent the 4th U.S. Cavalry to flank to the east and gathered what he could of the 7th Pennsylvania Cavalry to repeat the charge. About 150 Pennsylvanians galloped down the Murfreesboro Road toward the courthouse. "As we neared the square, their cavalry fled precipitately, after firing a few scattering shots, and their artillery following, the pursuit commenced," recalled Sipe. The 4th U.S. Cavalry and 7th Pennsylvania Cavalry hammered the column's rear as Wheeler's horsemen fled toward the Skullcamp Bridge. Two of Wheeler's cannons were captured along the way. Many Confederates had reached safety across the Duck when the wheels of another cannon broke through the bridge deck, partially blocking the way and inducing some panic among the Confederate horsemen. Wheeler led the 1st Confederate Cavalry back across the river, trying to save the situation. Just then, the 3rd Indiana Cavalry charged in with drawn sabers.

This attack caught Wheeler's forces at their most vulnerable. The Confederates "fled in disorder near a half mile [eastward along the river] where, the commons narrowing into a lane, they must fight or be run down. They fought...desperately, using saber and clubbing muskets and pistols. The fight was hand-to-hand for 300 yards, when both parties plunged into the river. Even here we used the trusty saber with effect," recalled an Indianan. Generals Wheeler and Martin escaped by hurtling their horses into the swollen river and swimming for it under fire. Another 200 prisoners fell to the Union along the Duck River; nearly half of Wheeler's force (509 of 1,200 men) was captured at Shelbyville. Minty's brigade lost 50 casualties in this decisive victory for the Federal cavalry. The Federals did not pursue beyond the river.[185]

The Federals also moved along the Manchester Pike on June 27. That morning, the Lightning Brigade stormed into Manchester, surprising its small garrison and capturing the key town. Thomas's corps arrived throughout June 27, followed by McCook's men and Crittenden's XXI Corps the next day. By dusk on June 28, both armies were concentrated in their respective destinations—Rosecrans with forty thousand infantry at Manchester, and Bragg's thirty thousand infantry twelve miles south in Tullahoma's

Above: The Duck River as seen from the modern Skullcamp Bridge in 2011. An earlier bridge piling on the original site is visible. *Photograph by Terry R. Woodson.*

Left: Simon Bolivar Buckner. *Perryville Battlefield State Historic Site.*

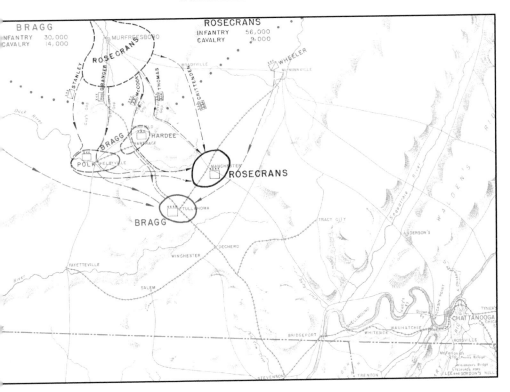

The Tullahoma Campaign through June 30. From *West Point Atlas of American Wars.* *Author's collection.*

fortifications. Granger's infantry remained along the Highland Rim, while Stanley's cavalry transferred from Shelbyville via Fairfield to Manchester. Wheeler's battered units regrouped around Tullahoma, while Forrest (who had forded the Duck River four miles downstream of Shelbyville) joined the Army of Tennessee during the day. Bragg also had reinforcements on the way: on the night of June 26, General Buckner started via rail from Knoxville with three thousand infantrymen.[186]

Federal probes discovered the nature of the Tullahoma fortifications and found that the Confederates were improving them. The rain had turned the flat and sandy terrain between Manchester and Tullahoma into a deep swamp, flooding both armies' camps. Rosecrans consulted his maps and realized that Bragg's supply line depended on the road and rail crossings over the Elk River at Estill Springs, seven miles southeast of Tullahoma. If those could be cut, Bragg would be isolated from Chattanooga. These bridges ultimately played a key role in both generals' strategies for the rest of the campaign.[187]

The road and rail bridges over the Elk River at Estill Springs, as seen in 2011. *Photograph by Terry R. Woodson.*

On June 28, Rosecrans sent the Lightning Brigade after the Army of Tennessee's lifeline. In a nod to the spring's tactics, John Beatty's infantry camped at Hillsborough to hold open the brigade's return route. Wilder's men rode for the Elk but found the water too high to ford. A Confederate infantry brigade, plus the first elements of Buckner's command arriving from Knoxville, thwarted Wilder's attempt to capture the bridges at Estill Springs. On June 29, the Lightning Brigade crossed the Elk via the bridge at Pelham and headed south toward Decherd, reaching there at 8:00 p.m. after a march over "streams that swam our smallest horses," recalled Wilder. After overpowering Decherd's garrison of eighty men, the Federals burned stores, cut Bragg's telegraph line to Chattanooga and destroyed three hundred yards of track using special tools that twisted the rails as they were removed. Hearing of Buckner's approach, Wilder drew away toward Pelham.

The next morning, June 30, the Federals tore up a branch line of the N&C leading toward Tracy City. Colonel Wilder also observed more of Buckner's troops arriving by train, along with cavalry under Forrest assembling at Decherd. "I deemed it impossible to accomplish anything further," he recalled. Wilder led his men out of the Confederate trap by feinting toward Chattanooga and scattering his regiments along several routes to rejoin the Federal army at Manchester. At noon on June 30, a wet and muddy. Wilder reported back to Thomas and Rosecrans, who seemed surprised to see him. Amazingly, the Lightning Brigade lost no men on this odyssey into Bragg's rear.[188]

While the Lightning Brigade wreaked havoc along the Elk, both sides deployed for a battle at Tullahoma. Hardee's Corps held the town's eastern fortifications, while Polk's infantry garrisoned the western lines. Thomas's XIV Corps slogged southward and deployed along Crumpton's Creek, a stream about five miles north of Tullahoma that represented the only major topographic change in the nearly flat land between Manchester and Tullahoma. McCook's men posted to the west, while Crittenden's men took position to the east. The Army of the Cumberland brushed against Wheeler's cavalry along the creek, causing some sharp skirmishing with Negley's and Brannan's troops on June 29 and 30. Rosecrans decided to flank Bragg and made plans to strike toward the Elk with Crittenden's corps on July 1.[189]

Despite its strong position, all was not well in the Army of Tennessee. General Bragg's health was breaking down, but he remained intent on making

The old Manchester-Tullahoma Road slopes down to Crumpton's Creek. This is a 2011 view looking southward from Thomas's position on the ridge. The creek runs in front of the far wood line. *Photograph by Terry R. Woodson.*

Rosecrans fight him at Tullahoma. Polk visited Bragg on the morning of June 29 and found him full of anticipation for a Federal attack on his earthworks. Bragg also admitted the Federal cavalry's superiority over his troopers, plus the fact that his supply line had been cut at Decherd and it might be again.[190]

Disturbed, Polk departed and found General Hardee. That afternoon, the two corps commanders secured an appointment with Bragg to discuss the situation. The army commander asked Polk's opinion of the state of affairs, and Polk responded that the Army of Tennessee needed to reopen its supply lines. Bragg gave the happy news that communications were again open. "How do you propose to maintain them?" challenged Polk. "By posting cavalry along the line," replied Bragg. Polk scoffed at this solution, predicting that Rosecrans would cut the road to Decherd "in less than thirty-six hours," according to an aide. Such an event would be a disaster for the army, and it might be surrounded or pushed into Alabama, leaving Chattanooga wide open. Three times Polk proposed retreat; Hardee voiced no opinion but did endorse the merit of Polk's views. In the end, Bragg deployed elements of Hardee's Corps to guard the road and railroad leading to the Elk River.[191]

The next day, Bragg changed his mind. At 3:00 p.m. on June 30, a mere twenty-four hours after he overruled Polk's pleas to pull back, Bragg ordered the bishop to "have your wagon train ready to move on Allisona [Estill Springs] by the road south of the rail as soon as Hardee's train is out of the way." This order meant one thing: retreat.

The army's logistical and administrative tail headed south that evening and into the night. Shortly before midnight on June 30, the Army of Tennessee's infantry evacuated Tullahoma and marched for the Elk River and Decherd. Wheeler's cavalry covered the withdrawal. As the Confederate horsemen left Tullahoma on the morning of July 1, in Pennsylvania the Army of the Potomac and Army of Northern Virginia opened the three-day Battle of Gettysburg, soon to rank as the Civil War's bloodiest engagement. By midday on July 1, Bragg's troops were across the Elk. The river's flooded condition prompted Bragg to consider defending along the shoreline. Hardee caught wind of this notion and confidentially proposed a meeting with Polk and Buckner "to save this army and its honor" and avoid fighting another battle under Bragg's command. The meeting never took place, as a defeated and exhausted Bragg ordered his army to Cowan on July 2.[192]

Thomas's Federals learned of the Confederate departure from citizens of Tullahoma. Elements of Brannan's, Reynolds's and Sheridan's divisions occupied the town, while Negley's men skirted Tullahoma's east side to engage Bragg's rearguard. John Beatty's brigade led the march and soon

The Elk River as seen in 2011, looking much like it did in 1863. *Photograph by Terry R. Woodson.*

caught up to the Confederates. "I...drove [them] point to point for seven miles," wrote Beatty. "The force opposed to us simply desired to retard pursuit; and whenever we pushed against it vigorously fell back." Both sides spent much of July 2 skirmishing along the Elk. Polk's Corps managed to destroy the road and rail bridges at Estill Springs, but Thomas's and Crittenden's Federals forced crossings upstream.[193]

Bragg contemplated defending in the mountains behind Cowan but instead decided to head for Chattanooga. His army executed its final retirement on July 3, guarded by Wheeler's horsemen. That same day, Grant and Pemberton first met to discuss Vicksburg's surrender, and Confederate infantry charged up Cemetery Ridge in a vain final bid for victory at Gettysburg. Sheridan's infantry division pressured Wheeler's cavalry along the eleven miles of road from the Elk to Cowan and then another six miles up to University Place. The Federal pursuit broke off there on July 4, the same day Pemberton surrendered Vicksburg to Grant. By July 6, most of Bragg's army had crossed the Tennessee, and the remainder concentrated around Chattanooga on July 9. The United States now controlled Middle Tennessee.[194]

Chapter 11
A Victory Overshadowed

The Army of the Cumberland came to rest around Tullahoma. The twelve days of rations in Federal wagons ran out on July 5, forcing a halt. Morgan's raiders cut the L&N in Kentucky on July 6, again interrupting Rosecrans's flow of supplies from Louisville. The N&C between Murfreesboro and Cowan required repair; the Cowan Tunnel was largely intact, a sign that Bragg's engineers did not have the required explosives to ensure its permanent destruction. Rosecrans also needed to build up his supplies before plunging into the barren mountain ranges around Chattanooga. A year after Buell left, the Federal army was back, but this time in greater force. Rosecrans also held the initiative; the Confederates in Chattanooga stood no chance of repeating an expedition into Kentucky.[195]

Rosecrans's conquest of the region between Murfreesboro and the Tennessee River had been amazingly cheap. In the eleven days of operations from June 24 to July 4, only 570 Federals were killed, wounded, captured or went missing. Bragg's army never fully tabulated its losses, but Confederate personnel returns on July 10 show an effective strength nearly 5,000 men lower than on June 20. Half of that number covered Morgan's raiders, who had departed on the expedition into Kentucky and beyond. The Federals captured more than 1,600 prisoners, while Stewart's division lost 181 men in battle at Hoover's Gap. Cleburne's division sustained 121 casualties at Liberty Gap, for a total of 302 killed and wounded for the two divisions during the fighting along the Highland Rim. The balance of the Army of Tennessee's losses (about 600) consisted of battle casualties, sick or deserters.[196]

On July 3, as his army trudged over the mountains toward the Tennessee River, Bragg wrote Johnston to explain what happened:

The N&C at Cowan in 2011, looking southeast at the Cumberland Plateau. The Cumberland Mountain Tunnel is one mile east of Cowan itself; the approaching train has just exited it and is headed for Tullahoma and Murfreesboro. *Photograph by Terry R. Woodson.*

My last advices to the department represented the enemy advancing upon us in heavy force. We were immediately ready to receive him, and offered him battle, but he declined, and while holding a strong position, which we could not successfully attack, threw a force to our right and rear by which he successfully assailed our communications. No adequate force could be placed at these several points along the line without too much reducing our main body. I accordingly withdrew to Tullahoma, and reached there just in time to prevent an attack upon its feeble garrison.

The enemy established himself again in strong position on the defensive, and moved another heavy column against our bridges over Elk River, now swollen by heavy rains. By making a rapid march and using the railroad successfully, we saved all our supplies, and crossed the Elk just before a heavy column appeared at the upper bridge. We were now back against the mountains, in a country affording us nothing, with a long line of railroad to protect, and half a dozen passes on the right and left by which our rear could be gained. In this position it was perfectly practicable for the enemy to destroy our means of crossing the Tennessee, and thus secure our ultimate destruction without a battle. Having failed to bring him to that issue, so much desired by myself and troops, I reluctantly yielded to the necessity imposed by my position

and inferior strength, and put the army in motion for the Tennessee River.
Should we succeed in crossing it successfully (and I hear of no formidable
pursuit up to this morning), the Tennessee will be taken as our line.

Four days later, Bragg reported to Richmond that his army was across the Tennessee. "Our movement was attended with trifling loss of men and materials," he concluded. Privately he admitted that Tullahoma was "a great disaster."[197]

In contrast, spirits were high among the exhausted and muddy Federals. Word of the victory at Gettysburg came on July 4, prompting artillery salutes throughout the Army of the Cumberland's camps. Three days later came news of Vicksburg's fall. Port Hudson surrendered on July 9, opening the Mississippi River to Federal control and cutting the Confederacy in two. Together these four operations—Gettysburg, Tullahoma, Vicksburg and Port Hudson—resulted in a major turning point in the Civil War.[198]

In the North, operations along the Mississippi and in Pennsylvania garnered most of the public's attention. Secretary of War Edwin M. Stanton reflected this mood when he queried Rosecrans, "You and your noble army now have the chance to give the finishing blow to the rebellion. Will you neglect the chance?" Rosecrans defended his army in a reply the same day:

Just received your cheering dispatch announcing the fall of Vicksburg and confirming the defeat of Lee. You do not appear to observe the fact that this noble army has driven the rebels from Middle Tennessee, of which my dispatches advised you. I beg in behalf of this army that the War Department may not overlook so great an event because it is not written in letters of blood. I have now to repeat, that the rebel army has been forced from its strong intrenched positions at Shelbyville and Tullahoma, and driven over the Cumberland Mountains. My infantry advance is within 16 miles and my cavalry advance within 8 miles of the Alabama line. No organized rebel force within 25 miles of there, nor on this side of the Cumberland Mountains.

This dispatch was correct; in eleven days, the Federal front line had moved sixty miles closer to Chattanooga. The Army of the Cumberland now controlled Middle Tennessee and threatened Chattanooga itself. Access to Alabama, Georgia and East Tennessee lay bare. The Tullahoma Campaign may have been overshadowed by the bloodier events in other theaters, but its impact was no less important to the war's course.[199]

A Victory Overshadowed

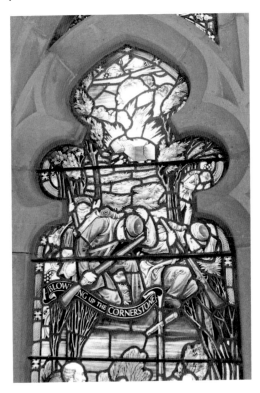

A stained-glass window in the University of the South's chapel commemorates the Federal destruction of the university cornerstone in July 1863. *Photograph by Terry R. Woodson.*

The victory at Tullahoma capped nine months of duels in Tennessee between United States and the Confederacy, from November 1862 to July 1863. William Starke Rosecrans and the Army of the Cumberland came of age during the Stones River and Tullahoma Campaigns. Rosecrans demonstrated himself to be a capable leader of men, able to create a solid command team and inspire his army. As a strategist and tactician, he proved able, although with a dangerous tendency to allow emotion to dominate his words and an attention to detail that caused him to sometimes forget the overall picture while directing his units. His personal battlefield leadership helped win the Battle of Stones River, while his development of Federal cavalry paid dividends in the spring and summer of 1863. Rosecrans's masterful Tullahoma movements dislodged and drove the Confederates from the Highland Rim to the Tennessee River.

By contrast, the operations in Middle Tennessee showed the limitations of Braxton Bragg as a commander. He proved a good organizer, but his unpredictable personality harmed relations with his subordinates. He failed to plan ahead, which led to missed opportunities at Stones River and along the Highland Rim. The paper war among the Army of Tennessee's high command wasted energy and stifled initiative among the officers. Bragg's combination of general operational passivity punctuated with bursts of activity only exacerbated the problems. The general's supporters point out, correctly, that he kept losing troops to other theaters in 1862 and 1863, but had his army been more active in its operations, Bragg would have retained them for use against Rosecrans. Erratic Confederate leadership both in and around the Army of Tennessee hampered that army's effectiveness and contributed to its failure to hold back the Federal advances from Nashville and Murfreesboro.

Militarily, the Stones River and Tullahoma Campaigns proved to be vital links in the chain of Federal advances from Louisville to Atlanta and beyond. The best approach route to Atlanta and the Deep South ran along the N&C from Nashville to Chattanooga, which meant that the United States had to control the area around Murfreesboro and Tullahoma to reach and hold Chattanooga or any territory beyond. The Confederate failure to hold Middle Tennessee opened access to the Deep South; the decisive campaigns of Chickamauga, Chattanooga and Atlanta would have been impossible without Stones River and Tullahoma.

These two campaigns also occurred during a critical political turning point for the North, when questions and policy shifts about emancipation, conscription, war weariness and even the Lincoln administration's viability gripped the United States. Success or failure on the battlefield affected the outcome of these debates. Good news from the Army of the Cumberland twice brightened Union prospects, especially in January 1863 after the failures at Fredericksburg and Vicksburg the preceding month. President Lincoln attested to Stones River's importance in a letter to Rosecrans in August 1863: "I can never forget, whilst I remember anything, that about the end of last year, and the beginning of this, you gave us a hard earned victory which, had there been a defeat instead, the nation could scarcely have lived over." The United States moved according to events outside Murfreesboro in December 1862 and January 1863, while successes near Tullahoma in June and July 1863 helped turn the Civil War's course.[200]

The Stones River and Tullahoma Campaigns now passed into the records. Having successfully conquered Middle Tennessee, General Rosecrans next turned his attention to dislodging Bragg's Confederates from Chattanooga. He paused for six weeks at Tullahoma to repair the railroad and build up supplies. On August 16, 1863, the Army of the Cumberland marched toward the Tennessee River to again do battle with the Army of Tennessee. The campaigns for Middle Tennessee were over; the battles for Chattanooga now commenced.[201]

Notes

CHAPTER 1

1. Noe, *Perryville*, 31; see also Daniel, *Days of Glory*.
2. Daniel, *Days of Glory*, 35, 43–45, 47, 56; Noe, *Perryville*, 10–14.
3. Noe, *Perryville*, 28–32; Parks, *General Edmund Kirby Smith CSA*, 198.
4. Harrison, *Civil War in Kentucky*, 23–32; see also Daniel, *Days of Glory*, 33–73.
5. Noe, *Perryville*, 19–20; a fine account of the battle can be found in Catton, *Grant Moves South*.
6. Daniel, *Days of Glory*, 75–106.
7. Noe, *Perryville*, 42–48.
8. Daniel, *Days of Glory*, 91–106.
9. Noe, *Perryville*, 48–62. Alexander McCook was Robert McCook's younger brother.
10. Ibid., 15–17; see also McWhiney, *Braxton Bragg and Confederate Defeat*, 1–173. McWhiney stated that Bragg was born at home, while Noe claimed that Bragg was born while his mother was in jail. Bragg's brother, Thomas, was governor of North Carolina from 1855 to 1859 and one of the state's U.S. senators in 1861 when the state seceded. He later served as Confederate attorney general in 1861 and 1862.
11. This and preceding paragraphs are taken from Kolakowski, *Civil War At Perryville*, 21–23.

CHAPTER 2

12. Unless otherwise noted, all sources for this chapter can be found in Kolakowski.

13. *The War of the Rebellion: A Compilation of the Official Records of the Union and Confederate Armies*, ser. I, vol. 16, pt. 2, 538, 554–55 (hereafter cited as *OR*, all from series I).

14. Davis, *Orphan Brigade*, 135–36.

15. Daniel, *Days of Glory*, 173–77; *OR*, vol. 16, pt. 1, 11–12. The name "Army of the Cumberland" will be used throughout.

CHAPTER 3

16. Lamers, *Edge of Glory*, 8–19.

17. Ibid., 182–83.

18. Sheridan, *Personal Memoirs of P.H. Sheridan*, 110; Daniel, *Days of Glory*, 182–83.

19. Durham, *Nashville*, 130–31.

20. McWhiney, *Braxton Bragg and Confederate Defeat*, 337–38.

21. Ibid., 323–36.

22. McWhiney, *Braxton Bragg and Confederate Defeat*, 274–81; Noe, *Perryville*, 54–58; see also Liddell, *Liddell's Record*, 101. Until his death in 1864, Polk remained bishop of Louisiana in addition to his military duties.

23. McWhiney, *Braxton Bragg and Confederate Defeat*, 274–81; Noe, *Perryville*, 54–58; Liddell, *Liddell's Record*, 101.

24. McWhiney, *Braxton Bragg and Confederate Defeat*, 344.

25. Symonds, *Joseph E. Johnston*, 187–96.

26. Now 6th Street, just south of Union Street.

27. Lamers, *Edge of Glory*, 181–89.

28. Ibid., 192; Durham, *Nashville*, 133–34.

29. McPherson, *Tried By War*, 142–60; Lamers, *Edge of Glory*, 194–95.

30. *OR*, vol. 20, pt. 1, 63–66; see also Duke, *History of Morgan's Cavalry*, 297–316.

31. *OR*, vol. 20, pt. 1, 44–51; see also Calkins, *History of the One Hundred and Fourth Regiment*, 46–60.

32. *OR*, vol. 20, pt. 1, 44–51; Calkins, *History of the One Hundred and Fourth Regiment*, 46–60.

33. *OR*, vol. 20, pt. 1, 44–51; Calkins, *History of the One Hundred and Fourth Regiment*, 46–60.

34. *OR*, vol. 20, pt. 1, 44–51; Calkins, *History of the One Hundred and Fourth Regiment*, 46–60.
35. *OR*, vol. 20, pt. 1, 44–51; Calkins, *History of the One Hundred and Fourth Regiment*, 46–60.
36. Duke, *History of Morgan's Cavalry*, 316–25.
37. McWhiney, *Braxton Bragg and Confederate Defeat*, 343–45.
38. Lamers, *Edge of Glory*, 199–201.

Chapter 4

39. *OR*, vol. 20, pt. 1, 663.
40. Ibid., 174–82, 205–6.
41. Noe, *Perryville*, 92–98.
42. Ibid.
43. *OR*, vol. 20, pt. 1, 371–72.
44. Ibid., 189–90.
45. Ibid., 371–72, 843, 957–59.
46. Ibid., 665, 672–73, 843.
47. Lamers, *Edge of Glory*, 204–7.
48. *OR*, vol. 20, pt. 1, 672–73.
49. Ibid., 190–91; see also Beatty, *Citizen Soldier*, 200–201.
50. *OR*, vol. 20, pt. 1, 672–73; Lamers, *Edge of Glory*, 211–17.
51. *OR*, vol. 20, pt. 1, 192; Lamers, *Edge of Glory*, 213–15.
52. *OR*, vol. 20, pt. 1, 664.
53. Ibid., 912–24; Symonds, *Stonewall of the West*, 107–8. As Cleburne's men marched, at the same time off Cape Hatteras, North Carolina, the USS *Monitor* sank in a gale.
54. Reinhart, *August Willich's Gallant Dutchmen*, 127–35; see also *OR*, vol. 20, 304–337, although some reports try to put the best face on Federal preparedness that morning. Confederate accounts noted passing camps with hastily abandoned breakfast and coffee still warm.
55. Reinhart, *August Willich's Gallant Dutchmen*, 127–35; *OR*, vol. 20, pt. 1, 304, 948.
56. Reinhart, *August Willich's Gallant Dutchmen*, 127–35; *OR*, vol. 20, pt. 1, 304, 948.
57. *OR*, vol. 20, pt. 1, 844, 857, 912.
58. Ibid., 270–78; a more impressionistic account can be found in Dodge, *Waif of the War*, 64–65.

59. *OR*, vol. 20, pt. 1, 844, 857, 912; Dodge, *Waif of the War*, 64–65; see also *OR*, vol. 20, pt. 1, 336–39.

60. Liddell, *Liddell's Record*, 108–9.

61. *OR*, vol. 20, pt. 1, 278, 876, 883, 893.

62. Ibid., 264.

63. Ibid., 337, 341, 912, 948; see also Liddell, *Liddell's Record*, 109.

64. Liddell, *Liddell's Record*, 109; Dodge, *Waif of the War*, 65–66; *OR*, vol. 20, pt. 1, 264–65, 270–71. Confederate reports made note that the 2nd Arkansas squared off with the 22nd Indiana as at Perryville and again got the best of the Federal unit.

CHAPTER 5

65. Lamers, *Edge of Glory*, 219–20; *OR*, vol. 20, pt. 1, 192–93, 448–49.

66. Lamers, *Edge of Glory*, 219–20; *OR*, vol. 20, pt. 1, 192–93, 448–49.

67. *OR*, vol. 20, pt. 1, 686–89, 754.

68. Sheridan, *Personal Memoirs of P.H. Sheridan*, 221; Losson, *Tennessee's Forgotten Warriors*, 81; see also Beaudot, *24th Wisconsin in the Civil War*, 148–70, and Allendorf, *Long Road to Liberty*, 77–79. Good accounts of Sill's death can be found also in Lambert, *Heroes of the Western Theater*, 139–42. In 1869, Sheridan named Fort Sill, Oklahoma, in memory of General Sill.

69. Sheridan, *Personal Memoirs of P.H. Sheridan*, 121–22.

70. Beaudot, *24th Wisconsin in the Civil War*, 164–65. Exactly seventy-five years after his father fought outside the city, MacArthur's son, General Douglas MacArthur, married Murfreesboro resident Jean Marie Faircloth in April 1937.

71. *OR*, vol. 20, pt. 1, 846–47, 949.

72. Ibid., 637, 966–67.

73. Beatty, *Citizen Soldier*, 201–2; see also Johnson, *That Body of Brave Men*, 274–82. A slightly different account can be found in Kirk Jenkins's excellent book on the 15th Kentucky called *The Battle Rages Higher*, published by the University Press of Kentucky.

74. *OR*, vol. 20, pt. 1, 377–78, 938–39.

75. Beatty, *Citizen Soldier*, 201–2; *OR*, vol. 20, pt. 1, 377–78; see also Jenkins, *Battle Rages Higher*.

76. Sheridan, *Personal Memoirs of P.H. Sheridan*, 123–24; see also *OR*, vol. 20, pt. 1, 431–33, 724–25, 763–67.

77. Beaudot, *24ᵗʰ Wisconsin in the Civil War*, 163; Johnson and Buel, *Battles and Leaders of the Civil War*, 609 (hereafter cited as "*3 B&L*").
78. Beatty, *Citizen Soldier*, 202–3; see also Johnson, *That Body of Brave Men*, and *OR*, vol. 20, pt. 1, 377–78.
79. Beaudot, *24ᵗʰ Wisconsin in the Civil War*, 167; *OR*, vol. 20, pt. 1, 407–8, 421, 727.
80. Lamers, *Edge of Glory*, 225–27, 247.
81. Johnson, *That Body of Brave Men*, 280–82; *OR*, vol. 20, pt. 1, 939.
82. Johnson, *That Body of Brave Men*, 282–84.
83. Ibid., 283–99, gives the best account of this action.

CHAPTER 6

84. *OR*, vol. 20, pt. 1, 777.
85. Ibid., 665–66, 782–90; see also Griggs, *General John Pegram C.S.A.*, 60–62.
86. *OR*, vol. 20, pt. 1, 724–25, 728–29.
87. Ibid., 243, 927–28, 948–49.
88. Ibid., 580, 927–28, 947; Lambert, *Heroes of the Western Theater*, 144.
89. Liddell, *Liddell's Record*, 111–13; *OR*, vol. 20, pt. 1, 502–3, 879–80.
90. Liddell, *Liddell's Record*, 111–13; *OR*, vol. 20, pt. 1, 597–98, 776–77, 879–80.
91. Sheridan, *Personal Memoirs of P.H. Sheridan*, 125; *OR*, vol. 20, pt. 1, 449, 460–62, 516–18.
92. *OR*, vol. 20, pt. 1, 516–18, 527–28; 710–11; see also Head, *Campaigns and Battles of the Sixteenth Regiment*, 100–110.
93. Sheridan, *Personal Memoirs of P.H. Sheridan*, 125; *OR*, vol. 20, pt. 1, 449, 460–62, 516–18, 690.
94. *OR*, vol. 20, pt. 1, 792–94.
95. Ibid., 545, 555–56, 838–39; Sheridan, *Personal Memoirs of P.H. Sheridan*, 126.
96. *OR*, vol. 20, pt. 1, 545, 690–91.
97. *OR*, vol. 20, pt. 1, 545; Neff, *Tennessee's Battered Brigadier*, 64–65; Johnson and Buel, *3 B&L*, 628–29.
98. Lamers, *Edge of Glory*, 232–33; Sheridan, *Personal Memoirs of P.H. Sheridan*, 126–27. Later, Rosecrans saved the buttons from his coat in an envelope marked "Buttons I wore the day Garesche was killed." Garesche was the highest-ranking Hispanic officer killed in the battle.
99. *OR*, vol. 20, pt. 1, 194.
100. Ibid.; see also Lamers, *Edge of Glory*, 233–37, and Sheridan, *Personal Memoirs of P.H. Sheridan*, 127–28.

101. *OR*, vol. 20, pt. 1, 662, 667.

102. Liddell, *Liddell's Record*, 113–14.

103. *OR*, vol. 20, pt. 1, 195, 667–68.

104. Ibid.

105. Ibid.; see also McWhiney, *Braxton Bragg and Confederate Defeat*, 366–70, and Neff, *Tennessee's Battered Brigadier*, 68–72. Pillow was the same man who had shamefully abandoned his army at Fort Donelson in February and was assigned to command Palmer's brigade two hours before the advance.

106. *OR*, vol. 20, pt. 1, 587–88, 786, 797–99; Fyffe is quoted in McDonough, "Last Day at Stones River," 8.

107. *OR*, vol. 20, pt. 1, 450–51, 455–56, 799, 812–13, 815, 833.

108. Ibid.; McWhiney, *Braxton Bragg and Confederate Defeat*, 366–70; see also Kimberly and Holloway, *Forty-First Ohio Veteran Volunteer Infantry*, 41–42, and Johnson and Buel, *3 B&L*, 607.

109. *OR*, vol. 20, pt. 1, 215, 674.

CHAPTER 7

110. Ibid., 700–702.

111. McWhiney, *Braxton Bragg and Confederate Defeat*, 371; *OR*, vol. 20, pt. 1, 669, 700–701.

112. McWhiney, *Braxton Bragg and Confederate Defeat*, 371; *OR*, vol. 20, pt. 1, 669, 700–701.

113. *OR*, vol. 20, pt. 1, 185–86; 196.

114. Lamers, *Edge of Glory*, 244–46. Circumstantial evidence for this view can be found in Rosecrans's actions and viewpoint after the Army of the Cumberland's other near-death experience at Chickamauga in September 1863. For details on Morgan's Christmas Raid against the L&N, see Gorin, *Morgan Is Coming!*, 65–97.

115. McWhiney, *Braxton Bragg and Confederate Defeat*, 374–76.

116. *OR*, vol. 20, pt. 1, 699.

117. Ibid., 683, 700–702.

118. *OR*, vol. 23, pt. 2, 613–24. Johnston cited a refusal to put himself forward in the 1850s over a colleague to back up his actions. He should have realized that his position was different now; it is one thing if a subordinate tears down a superior or equal to climb but quite another if a senior officer steps down to take over a junior's place.

119. *OR*, vol. 20, pt. 1, 698–99.

120. Ibid., 663–971. See especially the reports of Bragg, Polk, Hardee, Breckinridge, McCown and attached correspondence.
121. McWhiney, *Braxton Bragg and Confederate Defeat*, 380–89; Symonds, *Joseph E. Johnston*, 195–201.
122. *OR*, 16 pt. 1, 1,097–1,113.
123. Ibid., 1,101–3.

CHAPTER 8

124. Lamers, *Edge of Glory*, 244–49; Jenkins, *Battle Rages Higher*, 119–21. During the winter, Hazen's brigade veterans raised funds and constructed a large stone monument next to the Round Forest to commemorate their stand on December 31. The brigades' dead were buried at its foot. Today, the Hazen Monument is the oldest Civil War monument still in its original location.
125. Lamers, *Edge of Glory*, 250; Sheridan, *Personal Memoirs of P.H. Sheridan*, 92–93. Granger's force was formally known as the Army of Kentucky until June 8, 1863, when it became the Reserve Corps.
126. Lamers, *Edge of Glory*, 248–49.
127. Daniel, *Days of Glory*, 249–51; Jenkins, *Battle Rages Higher*, 120–25.
128. Daniel, *Days of Glory*, 251–57; Lamers, *Edge of Glory*, 258–60, 267–68.
129. Lamers, *Edge of Glory*, 253–54; Baumgartner, *Blue Lighting*, 33–78. Wilder was the same man who had surrendered Munfordville on September 17, 1862.
130. Lamers, *Edge of Glory*, 252–63; Daniel, *Days of Glory*, 233–54. In the event, Grant won the commission thanks to his capture of Vicksburg in July 1863.
131. *OR*, vol. 23, pt. 2, 623–26, 759.
132. Symonds, *Joseph E. Johnston*, 194–95; see also Jones, "Tennessee and Mississippi," 134–47.
133. Symonds, *Joseph E. Johnston*, 194–95; Jones, "Tennessee and Mississippi," 134–47. General Van Dorn was a West Point classmate of Rosecrans's.
134. Fremantle, *Three Months in the Southern States*, 137–64.
135. Bradley, *Tullahoma*, 19–40; Daniel, *Days of Glory*, 237–42; *OR*, vol. 23, pt. 1, 1–2.
136. Duke, *History of Morgan's Cavalry*, 348; Gorin, *Morgan Is Coming!*, 99–104; *OR*, vol. 23, pt. 1, 65, 151–60.
137. *OR*, vol. 23, pt. 1, 73–126, 182–83, 187–89, 219.

138. Daniel, *Days of Glory*, 237.

139. Lamers, *Edge of Glory*, 257–58; *OR*, vol. 23, pt. 1, 281–95.

140. For the best book on the battle, see Furgurson, *Chancellorsville*.

141. Catton, *Grant Moves South*, 407–449; Jones, "Tennessee and Mississippi," 134–47; *OR*, vol. 23, pt. 1, 585.

142. Lamers, *Edge of Glory*, 266–70.

143. Ibid.; Fremantle, *Three Months in the Southern States*, 137–38, 161–62. In Fremantle's words, Bragg's men "received" Vallandigham "in the capacity of a destitute stranger. They do not in any way receive him officially, and it does not suit the policy of either party to be identified with one another."

144. Lamers, *Edge of Glory*, 269–72.

145. Bradley, *With Blood and Fire*, 13–38; Daniel, *Days of Glory*, 242–45; Sheridan, *Personal Memoirs of P.H. Sheridan*, 134–35.

146. *OR*, vol. 23, pt. 1, 10.

147. Ibid.

CHAPTER 9

148. Bradley, *Tullahoma*, 32–37; *OR*, vol. 23, pt. 1, 404–5; Arbuckle, *Cowan Pusher District*, passim. Governor Isham Harris was from the Winchester area. Winchester and Franklin County ranked among the most pro-secessionist parts of Tennessee, while Shelbyville was a highly pro-Union town. During the war, Estill Springs was also known as Allisona.

149. *OR*, vol. 23, pt. 1, 585. Bragg's strength return for June 20, 1863, can be confusing, for it shows an effective strength of forty-three thousand yet a total present of fifty-five thousand. The balance is made up of administrative troops, those in hospital and other such personnel who are not considered available for combat. Effective strengths will be used for Bragg's army, although this tail of twelve thousand men should be noted when considering Bragg's movements during the Tullahoma Campaign.

150. Ibid.; *OR*, vol. 23, pt. 2, 440; see also Ridley, *Journals and Sketches of the Army of Tennessee*, 180–81, and Gorin, *Morgan Is Coming!*, 99–109.

151. *OR*, vol. 23, pt. 1, 404–5; Lamers, *Edge of Glory*, 277–79; Daniel, *Days of Glory*, 265–67.

152. *OR*, vol. 23, pt. 1, 404–5; Lamers, *Edge of Glory*, 277–79; Daniel, *Days of Glory*, 265–67. The strengths come from the returns of June 30, 1863, in *OR*, vol. 23, pt. 1, 410–11.

153. Reinhart, *History of the 6ᵗʰ Kentucky Volunteer Infantry*, 193; see also the reports from XXI Corps in *OR*, vol. 23, pt. 1, 521–32.

154. Baumgartner, *Blue Lighting*, 84–87; *OR*, vol. 23, pt. 1, 430–32.

155. *OR*, vol. 23, pt. 1, 601–2, 611.

156. Ibid., 457–58.

157. Ibid.

158. *OR*, vol. 23, pt. 1, 601–2, 611; *Confederate Veteran* 33, 100–101.

159. *OR*, vol. 23, pt. 1, 601–2, 611; *Confederate Veteran* 33, 100–101; see also *OR*, vol. 23, pt. 1, 458–59; Baumgartner, *Blue Lighting*, 88–92.

160. *OR*, vol. 23, pt. 1, 601–2, 611; *Confederate Veteran* 33, 100–101; *OR*, vol. 23, pt. 1, 458–59; Baumgartner, *Blue Lighting*, 88–92.

161. *OR*, vol. 23, pt. 1, 483–87. Sheridan's division led the march from Murfreesboro on June 24, but it halted to guard the Shelbyville Road while Johnson's and Davis's divisions turned onto the Liberty Pike.

162. Ibid.

163. *OR*, vol. 23, pt. 1, 588, 594–95, 599–600.

164. Ibid., 483–87, 588, 594–95, 599–600.

165. *OR*, vol. 23, pt. 1, 521–31; Johnson and Buel, *3 B&L*, 637.

166. *OR*, vol. 23, pt. 1, 406, and pt. 2, 449–50. Rosecrans's exact phrase in his report is "As it was not yet certain whether the enemy would advance to test our strength on McCook's front, or mass on the flank of the Fourteenth Corps, near Fairfield, the orders for June 25 were as follows: 'Major-General Crittenden to advance to Lumley's Stand, 6 miles east of Beech Grove, and open communication with General Thomas. General Thomas to attack the rebels on the flank of his advance position at the forks of the road, and drive the rebels toward Fairfield. General McCook to feign an advance, as if in force on the Wartrace road, by the Liberty Gap passes. General Stanley, with his cavalry, to occupy their attention at Fosterville, and General Granger to support him with his infantry at Christiana.'"

167. Dodge, *Waif of the War*, 82–83; *OR*, vol. 23, pt. 1, 465–66.

168. *Confederate Veteran* 6, 430; Dodge, *Waif of the War*, 82–84; *OR*, vol. 23, pt. 1, 466, 472, 479–80, 487–89, 589–91.

169. *OR*, vol. 23, pt. 1, 406, 603–4. Matt's Hollow was named for local resident Matthew Martin, who was serving in the 23ʳᵈ Tennessee of Bushrod Johnson's brigade.

170. Ibid.; see also *OR*, vol. 23, pt. 2, 457–59.

CHAPTER 10

171. *OR*, vol. 23, pt. 2, 883.

172. *OR*, vol. 23, pt. 1, 431, 435.

173. Ibid., 431, 435, 459, 604–6; *OR*, vol. 23, pt. 2, 884; Gould and Kennedy, *Memoirs of a Dutch Mudsill*, 143–44; see also Johnson, *That Body of Brave Men*, 362–67.

174. *OR*, vol. 23, pt. 1, 533, 618.

175. Ibid.

176. For a divergent view, see Steven Woodworth's "Braxton Bragg and the Tullahoma Campaign" in Woodworth, *Art of Command*, 163–67. Bragg should have reinforced Polk with Wheeler's and Forrest's cavalry to protect his flank and distract Stanley's Federal horsemen.

177. The best example of an army reacting to a Federal offensive while defending a natural barrier is the Army of Northern Virginia in May 1864 along the Rapidan River. Robert E. Lee and his officers had planned, mapped and reconnoitered possible countermoves against an offensive by the Army of the Potomac. Lee also enjoyed good communication and cooperation with his cavalry. When the Federals crossed the river on May 3, Lee quickly moved east and caught his opponents in the Wilderness, starting a two-day battle on May 5 and 6, 1864. This was the second time Lee's forces faced this problem: a year earlier, they had defended along the Rappahannock outside Fredericksburg and had been surprised by a Federal turning movement in late April 1863; through good teamwork, staff work and communication, Lee's army swiftly reacted and won the Battle of Chancellorsville.

178. *OR*, vol. 23, pt. 1, 583, 618; see also *OR*, vol. 23, pt. 2, 886. Bragg later explained his thinking to Richmond on June 27: "Yesterday the enemy in large force passed my right after skirmishing sharply along my whole front for two days. The line of Shelbyville being too long to be held successfully by my force, I today resumed my position in my intrenchments at this place to await the full developments."

179. Liddell, *Liddell's Record*, 128–29; *OR*, vol. 23, pt. 1, 608, 619.

180. Liddell, *Liddell's Record*, 128–29; *OR*, vol. 23, pt. 1, 608, 619; *OR*, vol. 23, pt. 2, 888; Head, *Campaigns and Battles of the Sixteenth Regiment*, 112–13. John Savage had resigned as colonel of the 16th Tennessee in March 1863.

181. *OR*, vol. 23, pt. 1, 536–37, 539–40, 556–67; see also Bradley, *Tullahoma*, 76–80.

182. *OR*, vol. 23, pt. 1, 536–37, 539–40, 556–67; Bradley, *Tullahoma*, 76–80. The 1ˢᵗ Middle Tennessee was recruited partly from Shelbyville; the area was so pro-Union it was known as "Little Boston."

183. *OR*, vol. 23, pt. 1, 536–37, 539–40, 556–67; Bradley, *Tullahoma*, 76–80.

184. *OR*, vol. 23, pt. 1, 536–37, 539–40, 556–67; Bradley, *Tullahoma*, 76–80.

185. *OR*, vol. 23, pt. 1, 536–37, 539–40, 556–67; Bradley, *Tullahoma*, 76–80. The Federals also liberated spy Pauline Cushman, who had been imprisoned in Shelbyville and was scheduled for execution.

186. *OR*, vol. 23, pt. 2, 885, 887; see also Baumgartner, *Blue Lighting*, 92–93. June 28, 1863, is the day when Major General Joseph Hooker was relieved by Major General George Meade as commander of the Army of the Potomac.

187. *OR*, vol. 23, pt. 1, 407; Gould and Kennedy, *Memoirs of a Dutch Mudsill*, 145–46.

188. *OR*, vol. 23, pt. 1, 431, 459–60; Baumgartner, *Blue Lighting*, 92–96. Some historians have claimed that General Thomas ordered the raid, but Thomas's report clearly states that Wilder's brigade moved "in compliance with department orders," meaning Rosecrans.

189. *OR*, vol. 23, pt. 1, 407–8, 426–28, 431–32, 608; Beatty, *Citizen Soldier*, 287–89.

190. *OR*, vol. 23, pt. 1, 621.

191. Ibid., 621–22.

192. Ibid., 622–24.

193. Beatty, *Citizen Soldier*, 290–91.

194. Sheridan, *Personal Memoirs of P.H. Sheridan*, 142–45; *OR*, vol. 23, pt. 1, 583–84, 615–17, 624–27. University Place is now known as Sewanee and was designated as the future University of the South. Leonidas Polk had consecrated the university's cornerstone in 1860. According to school lore, some of Sheridan's infantry destroyed the cornerstone on July 6.

CHAPTER 11

195. Lamers, *Edge of Glory*, 288–90; Gorin, *Morgan Is Coming!*, 238. The Confederate government in July 1863 inquired about possibly making another Kentucky expedition as in 1862, but the forces in East Tennessee and Chattanooga were too weak, while the Federal forces in Kentucky and Middle Tennessee were much stronger than in 1862.

196. *OR*, vol. 23, pt. 1, 403, 424, 425, 585–86, 587, 592, 610, 614.

197. Ibid., 584; Hallock, *Braxton Bragg and Confederate Defeat*, 23.
198. Lamers, *Edge of Glory*, 290–91.
199. *OR*, vol. 23, pt. 2, 518.
200. Basler, *Collected Works of Abraham Lincoln*, 424–25.
201. Lamers, *Edge of Glory*, 292–301.

Bibliography

Books

Allendorf, Donald. *Long Road to Liberty: The Odyssey of a German Regiment in the Yankee Army*. Kent, OH: Kent State Press, 2006.

Arbuckle, J.W. *Cowan Pusher District and Tunnel*. Winchester, TN: Herald-Chronicle, n.d.

Basler, Roy P., ed. *The Collected Works of Abraham Lincoln*. Volume 6. New Brunswick, NJ: Rutgers Press, 1953.

Baumgartner, Richard A. *Blue Lighting: Wilder's Mounted Infantry Brigade in the Battle of Chickamauga*. Huntington, WV: Blue Acorn, 2007.

Beatty, John. *The Citizen Soldier*. Cincinnati, OH: Wilstach, Baldwin & Company, 1879.

Beaudot, William J.K. *The 24th Wisconsin in the Civil War: The Biography of a Regiment*. Mechanicsburg, PA: Stackpole, 2003

Bennett, L.G., and William M. Haigh. *History of the Thirty-Sixth Regiment Illinois Volunteers During the War of the Rebellion*. Aurora, IL: Knickerbocker, 1876.

Bradley, Michael R. *Tullahoma: The 1863 Campaign for the Control of Middle Tennessee*. Shippensburg, PA: Burd Street Press, 2000.

————. *With Blood and Fire: Life Behind Union Lines in Middle Tennessee, 1863–65*. Shippensburg, PA: Burd Street Press, 2003.

Calkins, William Wirt. *The History of the One Hundred and Fourth Regiment of Illinois Volunteer Infantry*. Chicago: Donohue & Henneberry, 1895.

Catton, Bruce. *Grant Moves South*. Boston: Little Brown, 1960.

Connelly, Thomas L. *Civil War Tennessee*. Knoxville: University of Tennessee Press, 1979.

Cozzens, Peter. *No Better Place to Die: The Battle of Stones River*. Chicago: University of Illinois Press, 1990.

Daniel, Larry. *Days of Glory: The Army of the Cumberland*. Baton Rouge: Louisiana State University Press, 2004.

Davis, William C. *The Orphan Brigade*. Baton Rouge: Louisiana State University Press, 1980.

Davis, William C., ed. *Diary of a Confederate Soldier: John S. Jackman of the Orphan Brigade*. Columbia: University of South Carolina Press, 1990.

Dodge, W. Sumner. *A Waif of the War; or, the History of the Seventy-Fifth Illinois Infantry, Embracing the Entire Campaigns of the Army of the Cumberland*. Chicago: Church and Goodman, 1866.

Duke, Basil W. *A History of Morgan's Cavalry*. Bloomington: Indiana University Press, 1960.

Durham, Walter T. *Nashville: The Occupied City, 1862–63*. Knoxville: University of Tennessee Press, 2008.

Dykeman, Wilma. *Tennessee: A History*. Newport, TN: Wakestone, 1984.

Elliott, Sam Davis. *Soldier of Tennessee: General Alexander P. Stewart and the Civil War in the West.* Baton Rouge: Louisiana State University Press, 1999.

Fitch, Michael H. *Echoes of the Civil War as I Hear Them.* New York: RF Fenno, 1905.

Fowler, John D. *Mountaineers in Gray.* Knoxville: University of Tennessee Press, 2004.

Fremantle, A.J.L. *Three Months in the Southern States.* London: William Blackwood & Sons, 1863.

Furgurson, Ernest B. *Chancellorsville.* New York: Vintage, 1993.

Gorin, Betty J. *Morgan Is Coming! Confederate Raiders in the Heartland of Kentucky.* Prospect, KY: Harmony House, 2006.

Gould, David, and James P. Kennedy, eds. *Memoirs of a Dutch Mudsill: The War Memories of John Henry Otto.* Kent, OH: Kent State University Press, 2004.

Griggs, Walter S. *General John Pegram C.S.A.* Lynchburg, VA: H.E. Howard, 1993.

Hallock, Judith Lee. *Braxton Bragg and Confederate Defeat.* Volume 2. Tuscaloosa: University of Alabama Press, 1991.

Harrison, Lowell. *The Civil War in Kentucky.* Lexington: University Press of Kentucky, 1975.

Head, Thomas A. *Campaigns and Battles of the Sixteenth Tennessee Volunteers.* Nashville, TN: Cumberland Presbyterian, 1885.

Hennessy, John. *Return to Bull Run.* New York: Simon & Schuster, 1993.

Hoffman, Mark. *My Brave Mechanics: The First Michigan Engineers and Their Civil War.* Detroit, MI: Wayne State University Press, 2007.

Jenkins, Kirk. *The Battle Rages Higher.* Lexington: University Press of Kentucky, 2003.

Johnson, Mark W. *That Body of Brave Men: The U.S. Regular Infantry and the Civil War in the West.* Cambridge, MA: Da Capo, 2003.

Johnson, Robert Underwood, and Clarence Clough Buel, eds. *Battles and Leaders of the Civil War.* Volume 3. New York: Century Company, 1887.

Kimberly, Robert L., and Ephraim Holloway. *The Forty-First Ohio Veteran Volunteer Infantry in the War of the Rebellion.* Cleveland, OH: W.R. Smellie, 1897.

Kolakowski, Christopher L. *The Civil War at Perryville: Battling for the Bluegrass.* Charleston, SC: The History Press, 2009.

Lambert, Lois J. *Heroes of the Western Theater: 33d Ohio Veteran Volunteer Infantry.* Milford, OH: Little Miami, 2008.

Lamers, William M. *The Edge of Glory: A Biography of General William S. Rosecrans, U.S.A.* Baton Rouge: Louisiana State University Press, 1999.

Landt, Sophronius. *Your Country Calls.* Green Lake, WI: New Past, 2003.

Liddell, St. John R. *Liddell's Record.* Dayton, OH: Morningside, 1985.

Losson, Christopher. *Tennessee's Forgotten Warriors: Frank Cheatham and His Confederate Division.* Knoxville: University of Tennessee Press, 1989.

Manchester, William. *American Caesar.* Boston: Little, Brown, 1978.

McPherson, James M. *Tried by War: Abraham Lincoln as Commander in Chief.* New York: Penguin Publishing, 2009.

McWhiney, Grady. *Braxton Bragg and Confederate Defeat.* Vol. 1, *Field Command.* New York: Columbia University Press, 1969.

Murfin, James V. *The Gleam of Bayonets.* Baton Rouge: Louisiana State University Press, 2004.

Neff, Robert O. *Tennessee's Battered Brigadier: The Life of General Joseph B. Palmer CSA.* Franklin, TN: Hillsboro Press, 2000.

Noe, Kenneth. *Perryville: This Grand Havoc of Battle.* Lexington: University Press of Kentucky, 2002.

Parks, Joseph H. *General Edmund Kirby Smith CSA.* Baton Rouge: Louisiana State University Press, 1982.

Pendergast, Timothy. *Pen Pictures from the 2nd Minnesota.* Roseville, MN: PGB, 1998.

Powell, David A., and David A. Friedrichs. *The Maps of Chickamauga.* New York: Savas Beatie, 2009.

Reinhart, Joseph R. *August Willich's Gallant Dutchmen.* Kent, OH: Kent State University Press, 2006.

———. *A History of the 6th Kentucky Volunteer Infantry U.S.* Louisville, KY: Beargrass Press, 2000.

Ridley, Bromfield L. *Battles and Sketches of the Army of Tennessee.* Mexico, MO: Missouri Printing, 1906.

Sheridan, Philip H. *Personal Memoirs of P.H. Sheridan.* Cambridge, MA: Da Capo, 1992.

Smith, Lanny Kelton. *The Stones River Campaign: The Army of Tennessee.* Murfreesboro, TN: private printing, 2010.

———. *The Stones River Campaign: The Union Army.* Murfreesboro, TN: private printing, 2010.

Stewart, Nixon B. *Dan McCook's Regiment: 52nd O.V.I.* Alliance, OH: Review, 1900.

Symonds, Craig L. *Joseph E. Johnston: A Civil War Biography.* New York: Norton, 1992.

———. *Stonewall of the West: Patrick Cleburne and the Civil War.* Lawrence: University of Kansas Press, 1997.

U.S. War Department. *The War of the Rebellion: A Compilation of the Official Records of the Union and Confederate Armies.* 128 vols. Washington, D.C.: Government Printing Office, 1890–1901.

Woodworth, Steven E., ed. *The Art of Command in the Civil War.* Lincoln: University of Nebraska Press, 1998.

ARTICLES

Jones, Archer. "Tennessee and Mississippi, Joe Johnston's Strategic Problem." *Tennessee Historical Quarterly* 18, no. 2 (June 1959).

McDonough, James L. "The Last Day at Stones River—Experiences of a Yank and a Reb." *Tennessee Historical Quarterly* 40, no. 1 (Spring 1981).

PERIODICALS

Confederate Veteran.
National Tribune.

UNPUBLISHED PRIMARY SOURCES

Stones River National Battlefield Collections.

About the Author

C hristopher L. Kolakowski was born and raised in Fredericksburg, Virginia. He received his BA in history and mass communications from Emory and Henry College and his MA in public history from the State University of New York–Albany. Chris has spent his career interpreting and preserving American military history with the National Park Service, the New York State government, the Rensselaer County (NY) Historical Society, the Civil War Preservation Trust, Kentucky State Parks and the Army Reserve. He has written and spoken on the Civil War, American Revolution, Napoleonic Wars and the wars of the twentieth century. In 2009, The History Press published his first book, *The Civil War at Perryville: Battling for the Bluegrass*. Today Chris currently works as a historian in Louisville, Kentucky.

Visit us at
www.historypress.net